BERLITZ®

ARABIC
FOR TRAVELLERS

By the staff of Editions Berlitz

Library of Congress Catalog Card Number: 74-1978

10th printing 1983

Printed in Switzerland

Editions Berlitz
1, avenue des Jordils
1000 Lausanne 6, Switzerland

$ From New York	£ From London
Total units ______	Total units ______
at $9.95 each	at £5.95
Total amount enclosed $ ______	Total amount enclosed £ ______
(N.Y. residents add sales tax)	(VAT is included)

Name ____________________________

____

Address ____________________________

____

____

Please complete and return this order form to:

Traveller's
Shopping Service
3490 Lawson Blvd.
Oceanside, N.Y. 11572
U.S.A.

or

Traveller's
Shopping Service
8, Trident Way
Brent Road
Southall
Middlesex UB2 5LS
England

Please order Berlitz books through your bookseller. Should you encounter any difficulties, write directly to any of the distributors listed on the back cover.

11405

Preface

You are about to visit an Arabic-speaking country. Our aim is to give you a practical phrase book to help you on your trip. *Arabic for travellers* provides:

* all the phrases and supplementary vocabulary you will need on your trip
* a wide variety of tourist and travel facts, tips and useful information
* a complete phonetic transcription, showing you the pronunciation of all the words and phrases listed
* special sections showing the replies your listener might give to you—just hand him the book and let him point to the appropriate phrase. This is especially practical in certain difficult situations (doctor, car mechanic, etc.). It makes direct, quick and sure communication possible
* a logical system of presentation so that you can find the right phrase for the immediate situation
* quick reference through colour coding. The major features of the contents are on the back cover; a complete index is given inside.

These are just a few of the practical advantages. In addition, the book will prove a valuable introduction to life in the Arab world.

There is a comprehensive section on Eating Out, giving translations and explanations for pratically anything one might find on a menu in the Middle East; there is a complete Shopping Guide that will enable you to obtain virtually anything you want. Trouble with the car? Turn to the mechanic's manual with its dual-language instructions. Feeling ill? Our medical section provides the most rapid communication possible between you and the doctor.

To make the most of *Arabic for Travellers,* we suggest that you start with the "Guide to Pronunciation". Then go on to "Some Basic Expressions". This not only gives you a minimum vocabulary, it helps you to pronounce the language.

With the Arabic used in this book you can make yourself understood throughout the Middle East. Of course there are considerable differences in vocabulary and usage (see next page). That's why you will sometimes find alternatives for words given in brackets [ ]. If your listener cannot understand the first expression, try the alternative.

We are particularly grateful to Mr. Aly Hussein, Dr. Z. Mahfouz of the Berlitz Schools of Egypt, Mr. Habib Rahme and Mr. Shukri Taher for their help in the preparation of this book, and also to Dr. T.J.A. Bennett for his advice concerning the transliteration. We also wish to thank Egyptair for its assistance.

We shall be very pleased to receive any comments, criticisms and suggestions that you think may help us in preparing future editions. Thank you. Have a good trip.

Throughout this book, the symbols illustrated here indicate small sections where phrases have been compiled that your foreign listener might like to say to **you**. If you don't understand him, give him the book and let him point to the phrase in his language. The English translation is just beside it.

A very basic grammar

Classical Arabic is the language of the Koran and dates back to the 7th century. But it has changed through the centuries, and modern spoken Arabic varies greatly from country to country.

This book, destined principally for Egypt, Lebanon and Jordan—but equally useful for the rest of the Middle East—tries to steer a middle course between the spoken and the written (classical) language. When the same (spoken) word is used in all countries, we give that word as the most direct means of communication with the people. But when the word is different from one country to another, we've provided the written (classical) word which is necessarily the same in all countries. Sometimes, however, the classical word is unfamiliar and almost never used. In this case you'll find the Egyptian word with the word(s) used in other countries in brackets [ ].

Arabic is a Semitic language and therefore differs structurally from English and European concepts of language. It is written from right to left.

GRAMMAR

Articles

The definite article (the) in Arabic is ال **(æl)** for both the masculine and feminine genders, and the singular and plural. It preceeds the noun and generally the adjective.

فندق	**fon**dok	hotel
كبير	kæ**bīr**	big
الفندق	æl **fon**dok	the hotel
الفندق الكبير	æl **fon**dok æl kæ**bīr**	the big hotel

There is no indefinite article (a/an). To give indefinite meaning the article is simply omitted.

GRAMMAR

Nouns

There are two genders, masculine and feminine. In general words ending in **æ** or **a** are feminine. The names of towns and countries are nearly always feminine.

	Masculine			Feminine	
طالب	tālib	student (m.)	طالبة	tālibæ	student (f.)
شارع	shǣri'	street	وردة	wærdæ	flower
دكان	dokkǣn	shop	فرنسا	faransa	France

There are two sorts of plurals in Arabic: one for two things (double), and another for three or more. Basically, to form the double add the ending ين **(ēn)** to a singular masculine noun, or تين **(tēn)** to a feminine noun. To make the plural for three or more, add the ending ين **(īn)** to singular masculine nouns and ات **(ǣt or āt)** to feminine nouns. There are, however, numerous exceptions and irregular plurals where the word changes, like the English "child" to "children". Here are a few examples:

Regular

فنان	fænnǣn	an artist	شجرة	shagara	a tree
فنانين	fænnǣnēn	two artists	شجرتين	shagartēn	two trees
فنانين	fænnǣnīn	artists	شجرات	shagarāt	trees

Irregular

ولد	wælæd	a boy	سمكة	sæmækæ	a fish
ولدين	wælædēn	two boys	سمكتين	sæmæktēn	two fish
أولاد	'æwlǣd	boys	سمك	sæmæk	fish

Adjectives

Adjectives do not come before the noun as in English, but afterwards. They agree with the noun in gender and number. Don't forget that when there is a definite article in front of the noun, the adjective must also be preceeded by the definite article. However, the verb "to be" doesn't exist in the present tense in Arabic. In order to describe something, just put the noun with the definite article, and then the adjective without the article.

البيت الكبير	æl bēt æl kæ**bīr**	the big house
البيت كبير .	æl bēt kæ**bīr**	The house is big.

When an adjective qualifies a plural noun that is not human, the adjective is put in the feminine singular.

شجرة كبيرة	shagara kæbīræ	a big tree
شجرات كبيرة	shagar**āt** kæbīræ	big trees

There are no possessive adjectives; instead a suffix is added to the noun. Here are the suffixes for masculine nouns (for feminine nouns insert the letter **t** shown in parentheses):

my	... ى	...(t)ī	our	... نا	...(t)nǣ
your(m.)	... ك	...(t)æk			
your(f.)	... ك	...(t)ik	your(pl.)	... كم	...(t)kom
his/its	... ه	...(t)oh			
her/its	... ها	...(t)hæ	their	... هم	...(t)hom

Adding a possessive pronoun suffix to a noun makes it definite, and therefore if an adjective follows, the adjective must have the definite article.

كتاب كبير	kit**ǣb** kæ**bīr**	a big book
كتابى الكبير	kit**ǣ**bī æl kæ**bīr**	my big book

Verbs

One particularity of Arabic verbs is that they change not only according to the subject (I, you, he, etc.), but also according to whether a man or a woman is spoken to. You'll find examples of this in "Some Basic Expressions" (pages 16–21). In the rest of this phrase book all verbs are given in the masculine form, unless the context shows clearly that you're addressing a woman.

The following is the past and present conjugation of the verb "to write". Note that the subject pronoun is normally omitted.

	Present tense		Past tense	
I	أكتب	**'æktob**	كتبت	**kætæbto**
you (m.)	تكتب	**tæktob**	كتبت	**kætæbtæ**
you (f.)	تكتبى	**tæktobī**	كتبتى	**kætæbti**
he/it	يكتب	**yæktob**	كتب	**kætæbæ**
she/it	تكتب	**tæktob**	كتبت	**kætæbæt**
we	نكتب	**næktob**	كتبنا	**kætæbnǣ**
you	تكتبوا	**tæktobū**	كتبتوا	**kætæbtū**
they	يكتبوا	**yæktobū**	كتبوا	**kætæbū**

To form the future tense, add the prefix سا **(sæ)** to the present tense.

When you want to make a negative sentence, put ما **(mǣ)** in front of the verb:

أنا أكتب .	**ænǣ 'æktob**	I write.
أنا ما أكتب .	**ænǣ mǣ 'æktob**	I don't write.

To ask a question, simply put هل **(hæl)** at the beginning of the sentence:

البيت كبير .	**æl bēt kæbīr**	The house is big.
هل البيت كبير ؟	**hæl æl bēt kæbīr**	Is the house big?

Personal pronouns

I	أنا	**ænǣ**	we	نحن	**næḥno**
you (m.)	أنت	**'intæ**			
you (f.)	انت	**'inti**	you	أنتم	**'æntom**
he/it	هو	**howæ**			
she/it	هى	**hiyæ**	they	هم	**hom**

GRAMMAR

Guide to pronunciation

Here are the 28 characters which comprise the Arabic alphabet. A character may have different forms, depending on whether it's used by itself or comes at the end, in the middle or at the beginning of a word.

Isolated	Final	Median	Initial	Name
ا	ـا			'ælif
ب	ـب	ـبـ	بـ	bi
ت	ـت	ـتـ	تـ	ti
ث	ـث	ـثـ	ثـ	si
ج	ـج	ـجـ	جـ	gim
ح	ـح	ـحـ	حـ	ḥa
خ	ـخ	ـخـ	خـ	kha
د	ـد			dæl
ذ	ـذ			zæl
ر	ـر			ri
ز	ـز			zēn
س	ـس	ـسـ	سـ	sin
ش	ـش	ـشـ	شـ	shin
ص	ـص	ـصـ	صـ	sād
ض	ـض	ـضـ	ضـ	da
ط	ـط	ـطـ	طـ	ta
ظ	ـظ	ـظـ	ظـ	za
ع	ـع	ـعـ	عـ	'ēn
غ	ـغ	ـغـ	غـ	gēn
ف	ـف	ـفـ	فـ	fi
ق	ـق	ـقـ	قـ	kāf
ك	ـك	ـكـ	كـ	kæf
ل	ـل	ـلـ	لـ	læm
م	ـم	ـمـ	مـ	mim
ن	ـن	ـنـ	نـ	nūn
ه ة	ـه ـة	ـهـ	هـ	hi
و	ـو			wāw
ي	ـي	ـيـ	يـ	yi

This, of course, is not enough to pronounce Arabic. We're offering you a helping hand by providing a transcription throughout this book. This and the following section are intended to make you familiar with our transcription and to help you get used to the sounds of Arabic.

As a minimum vocabulary for your trip, we've selected a number of basic words and phrases under the title "Some Basic Expressions" (pages 16–21).

An outline of the sounds of Arabic

The traditional Arabic script is composed of consonants only and is written from right to left. A system of vowel signs (small marks above or below the characters), used mainly in the Koran, in poetry and in texts for beginners ensures proper pronunciation.

Written Arabic is fairly uniform. The spoken language, however, can differ considerably from one country to another or even among regions of the same country. We have based our transcription on the dialect used in most parts of Lower Egypt and especially in Cairo. This dialect is widely understood throughout the Middle East thanks to Egyptian films, radio and the recordings of popular artists. In addition, the Egyptian dialect is easier to learn than the others because some difficult sounds have been replaced by simpler ones, so that several letters of the alphabet are pronounced alike.

You'll find the pronunciation of the Arabic letters and sounds explained below, as well as the symbols we use for them in the transcriptions. Of course, the sounds of any two languages are never exactly the same; but if you follow carefully the indications supplied here, you'll have no difficulty in reading our transcriptions in such a way as to make yourself understood.

Letters written **bold** should be stressed (pronounced louder).

Consonants

Letter	Approximate pronunciation	Symbol	Example
ء أ	glottal stop*	ʼ	أرنب ʼærnæb
ب	like **b** in **boy**	b	باب bǣb
ت	like **t** in **ten**	t	تاج tǣg
ث	in classical Arabic, like **th** in **thin**; in spoken Arabic:		
	1) like **s** in **sit**	s	ثورة sawra
	2) like **t** in **ten**	t	ثور tōr
ج	1) like **g** in **get** (Egypt)	g	جميل gæmīl
	2) like **s** in **pleasure** (most other countries)	zh	جميل zhæmīl
ح	like **h** in **hoot**, but more "emphatic" and with slight friction in throat	ḥ	حديد ḥædīd
خ	like **ch** in Scottish **loch**	kh	خرج kharagæ
د	like **d** in **day**	d	دب dibb
ذ	in classical Arabic, like **th** in **then**; in spoken Arabic:		
	1) like **z** in **zebra**	z	ذكى zæki
	2) like **d** in **day**	d	ذهب dæhæb
ر	like **r** in rolled Scottish **r**	r	رجل rāgil

* This corresponds, in English, to the initial blocking of the throat before a vowel, as before the second o in "cooperate". It is also heard in the Cockney pronunciation of t in "water" (wa'er). In Arabic, the glottal stop can occur before a vowel *or* a consonant and even at the end of a word.

PRONUNCIATION

ز	like **z** in **z**ebra	z	زيت	zēt
س	like **s** in **s**it	s	سبب	sæbæb
ش	like **sh** in **sh**ine	sh	شمس	shæms
ص	like **s** in **s**un, pronounced with considerable "emphasis"	s	صبر	sabr
ض	like **d** in **d**uck, pronounced with "emphasis"	d	ضيف	dēf
ط	like **t** in **t**ough, pronounced with "emphasis"	t	طيارة	tayyāra
ظ	in classical Arabic, like **th** in **th**en; in spoken Arabic: like **z** in **z**ebra	z	ظريف	zarīf
ع	similar to glottal stop (see above)	'	رفيع	rafī'
غ	like a soft version of **ch** in Scottish lo**ch** (or like French pronunciation of **r** in "rue")	g	غالى	gǣli
ف	like **f** in **f**eed	f	فانوس	fænūs
ق	in classical Arabic, an "emphatic" **k**; in spoken Arabic: 1) like **k** in **k**ite	k	قلب	kalb
	2) glottal stop (see above)	'	قمر	'amar
ك	like **k** in **k**ite	k	كتاب	kitǣb
ل	like **l** in **l**et	l	لطيف	latīf
م	like **m** in **m**eet	m	ملبن	mælbæn
ن	like **n** in **n**eat	n	نرجس	nærgis
ه	like **h** in **h**ear, whatever its position in the word	h	هرم	haram
و	like **w** in **w**ell	w	ورد	wærd
ى	like **y** in **y**ell	y	يكتب	yæktob

PRONUNCIATION

Vowels

The letters ا, و and ى in the list above can also serve as vowels. In addition, Arabic has three vowel signs (َ, ُ, ِ); they occur either above or below the letter and are pronounced after the letter that carries the sign. In contemporary written Arabic—as in this book—the vowel signs are generally omitted. The context shows the reader which is the appropriate vowel he has to supply.

َ ا	1) like **a** in northern English hat or in American what (short)	a	صبر	sabr
	2) like **a** in car (long)	ā	طار	tār
	3) like **a** in can(short)	æ	كتب	kætæbæ
	4) like **a** in can, but long	ǣ	كتاب	kitǣb
ُ و	1) like **aw** in **raw**, but with the lips more tightly rounded; it sounds quite reminiscent of **oo** in **foot** (short)	o	بن	bonn
	2) like **ou** in **four** (long)	ō	يوم	yōm
	3) like **oo** in **boot** (long)	ū	نور	nūr
ى	1) like **i** in **sit** (short)	i	من	min
	2) like **ee** in **meet** (long)	ī	جميل	gæmīl
	3) like **ay** in **day**, but a pure vowel, not a diphthong (long)	ē	بيت	bēt

Note

1) Each symbol in our transcriptions should be pronounced as shown above, regardless of its position in the word; e.g., **s** always has—even between two vowels or at the end of a word—to be pronounced as in sit, not as in houses.

2) Any consonants written double must be pronounced long; e.g., **kk** should be pronounced like in thi**ck c**oat, **pp** like in lam**p p**ost, **ss** like in ma**ss s**urvey, etc.

Some basic expressions

Yes.	أيوه .	æywæ
No.	لا .	læ
Please.	من فضلك . *	min fadlak*
Thank you.	شكراً .	shokran
Thank you very much.	شكراً جزيلا .	shokran gæzīlæn
That's all right.	عفواً .	æfwæn

Greetings

Good morning.	صباح الخير .	sabāḥil khēr
Good afternoon.	نهارك سعيد . **	nahārak sæid**
Good evening.	مساء الخير .	masā'il khēr
Good night.	ليلة سعيدة .	lēlæ sæida
Good-bye.	مع السلامة .	mæ'æl sælǣmæ
See you later.	الى اللقاء .	ilæl lika'
This is Mr...	أقدم السيد . . .	okaddim assæyid
This is Mrs...	أقدم السيدة . . .	okaddim issæyidæ
This is Miss...	أقدم الآنسة . . .	okaddim il ǣnisæ

As pointed out in the grammar section, verbs in Arabic change their endings depending whether the person addressed is a man or a woman. In this section, the phrases said to a **man** are marked with one asterisk (*); those said to a **woman** are marked with two asterisks (**). Phrases not marked do not change.

I'm very pleased to meet you.	تشرّفنا .	tæsharrafna
How are you?	كيف حالك ؟ **	kæyfæ ḥǣlik**
Very well, thank you.	بخير .	bikhēr
And you?	وأنت ؟ **	wæ inti**
Fine.	كويسة . **	kwæyyisæ**
Excuse me.	آسفة .	'æsfæ

Questions

Where?	أين ؟	æynæ
Where's...?	أين . . . ؟	æynæ
Where are...?	أين . . . ؟	æynæ
When?	متى ؟	mætæ
What?	ما ؟	mæ
How?	كيف ؟	kæyfæ
How much?	كم ؟	kæm
How many?	كم ؟	kæm
Who?	من ؟	mæn
Why?	لماذا ؟	limǣzæ
Which?	أى . . . ؟	æyy
What do you call this?	ما اسم هذا ؟	mǣ ism hǣzæ
What do you call that?	ما اسم ذاك ؟	mǣ ism zǣk
What does this mean?	ما معنى هذا ؟	mæ mæ'nǣ hǣzæ
What does that mean?	ما معنى ذاك ؟	mǣ mæ'nǣ zǣk

Do you speak ... ?

Do you speak English?	هل تتكلم انجليزى ؟ *	hæl tætækællæm 'ingilīzi*
Do you speak German?	هل تتكلمى ألمانى ؟ **	hæl tætækællæmi 'almāni**
Do you speak French?	هل تتكلم فرنسى ؟ *	hæl tætækællæm firinsi*
Do you speak Spanish?	هل تتكلمى أسبانى ؟ **	hæl tætækællæmi 'æspǣni**
Do you speak Italian?	هل تتكلم ايطالى ؟ *	hæ tætækællæm 'itāli*
Could you please speak more slowly?	من فضلك تكلمى على مهلك . **	min fadlik tækællæmi 'ælǣ mæhlik**
Please point to the phrase in the book.	من فضلك أشر الى الجملة فى الكتاب . *	min fadlak æshir ilæl gomlæ fi æl kitǣb*
Just a minute. I'll see if I can find it in this book.	لحظة واحدة . سأبحث عنها فى الكتاب .	laḥza wǣḥidæ sæ'æb ḥæs 'ænhǣ fi æl kitǣb
I understand.	أنا أفهم .	ænæ æfhæm
I don't understand.	أنا لا أفهم .	ænæ lǣ æfhæm

Can ... ?

Can I have...?	أريد ... من فضلك ؟ *	orīd...min fadlak*
Can we have...?	نريد ... من فضلك ؟ **	norīd... min fadlik**
Can you show me...?	ممكن أن ترينى ... ؟ *	momkin æn torīni
Can you tell me...?	ممكن تقوليلى . . . ؟ **	momkin ti'ūlīli**
Can you please help me?	ممكن تساعدينى من فضلك ؟ **	momkin tisǣ'idīni min fadlik**

Wanting

I'd like...?	آريد ...	orīd
We'd like...?	نريد ...	norīd
Please give me...?	من فضلك اعطني . . . ؟ *	min fadlak a'tini*
Give it to me, please.	من فضلك اعطيهالى . **	min fadlik 'aatīhæ li**
Please bring me...	من فضلك احضرى لى... **	min fadlik ahdiri li**
Bring it to me, please.	من فضلك احضرها لى . *	min fadlak iḥdirhæ li*
I'm hungry.	أنا جعـانة .	ænæ gæ'æǣnæ
I'm thirsty.	أنا عطشان .	ænæ 'atshān
I'm tired.	أنا تعبـانة .	ænæ tææbæǣnæ
I'm lost.	أنا تهت .	ænæ toht
It's important.	انه مهم .	innæho mohim
It's urgent.	انه عاجل .	innæho æǣgil
Hurry up!	بسرعة !	bisor'æ

It is/There is...

It's...	انه ...	innæho
Is it...?	هل هو ... ؟	hæl howæ
It isn't...	انه ليس ...	innæho læysæ
There's/There are...	يوجد ...	yūgæd
Is there/Are there...?	هل يوجد ... ؟	hæl yūgæd
There isn't/There aren't...	لا يوجد ...	lǣ yūgæd
There isn't any/There aren't any.	لا يوجد منه .	lǣ yūgæd minho

A few common words

big/small	كبير / صغير	kæbīr/sagīr
quick/slow	سريع / بطيء	særī'/batī'
early/late	مبكر / متأخر	mobækkir/mit'akhkhar
cheap/expensive	رخيص / غالى	rakhīs/gǣlī
near/far	قريب / بعيد	karīb/bæ'īd
hot/cold	ساخن / بارد	sǣkhin/bǣrid
full/empty	مليان / فاضى	mælyæn/fādi
easy/difficult	سهل / صعب	sæhl/sa'b
heavy/light	ثقيل / خفيف	ti'īl/khæfīf
open/shut	مفتوح / مقفول	mæftūh/mæ'fūl
right/wrong	صحّ / غلط	saḥḥ/galat
old/new	قديم / جديد	'ædīm/gædīd
old/young	عجوز / شاب	'ægūz/shǣb
beautiful/ugly	جميل / وحش	gæmīl/wihish
good/bad	حسن / سيء	hæsin/sæyyi'
better/worse	أحسن / أسوأ	æhsæn/æswæ'

A few prepositions and some more useful words

at	عند	'indæ
on	على	ælæ
in	فى	fī
to	الى	'ilǣ
from	من	min
inside	داخل	fiddǣkhil
outside	خارج	fī æl khǣrig
up	فوق	fō'
down	تحت	tæḥt
before	قبل	kabl
after	بعد	bæ'd

with	مع	mæ'æ
without	بدون	bidūn
through	خلال	khilæl
towards	الى	'ilæ
until	حتى	ḥættæ
during	أثناء	'æsnæ'
and	و	wæ
or	أو	æww
not	ليس ـ غير	læysæ gēr
nothing	لا شيء	læ shæy'
none	ولا واحد	wælæ wæḥid
very	... جداً	...giddæn
also	كمان	kæmæn
soon	قريبا	karībæn
perhaps	ربما	robbæmæ
here	هنا	honæ
there	هناك	honæk
now	الآن	æl'æn
then	بعدين	bææden

Arrival

You've arrived. Whether you've come by ship or plane, you'll have to go through passport and customs formalities. You'll doubtless have received a customs-declaration form on board. Filling it in before landing will save you time upon arrival. (For car/border control, see page 145.)

There's certain to be somebody around who speaks English. That's why we're making this a brief section.

Passport control

Your travel agent probably helped you obtain a visa and told you about vaccination requirements for the countries you intend to visit. (Failure to comply with these procedures in advance may cause you unnecessary and time-consuming complications upon arrival in the Middle East.)

Here's my passport.	هذا جواز سفرى .	hǣzæ gæwǣz safari
I'll be staying...	سأبقى ...	sæ'abka
a few days	بضعة أيام	bid'at 'æyyǣm
a week	أسبوع	osbū
2 weeks*	أسبوعين	osbū'ēn
a month	شهر	shahr
I don't know yet.	لا أعرف بعد .	læ aarif bæ'd
I'm here on holidays.	أنا هنا فى أجازة .	ænǣ honǣ fi 'ægǣzæ
I'm here on business.	أنا هنا لشغل .	ænǣ honǣ li shogl
I'm just passing through.	أنا مارر من هنا بس .	ænǣ mǣrir min honæ bæss
I'm sorry, I don't understand. Is there anyone here who speaks English?	آسف لا أفهم . هل يوجد هنا أحد يتكلم الانجليزية ؟	ǣsif lǣ æfhæm. hæl yūgæd honæ æḥæd yætækællæm ingilīzi

* see grammar

Customs

After having your passport stamped by an immigration officer you'll go to customs. The customs officer will either have a quick look at your luggage or just ask what you have in addition to duty-exempt items. The chart below shows what you can bring in duty-free (all allowances are subject to change without notice).

	 Cigarettes		 Cigars		 (grams) Tobacco	 Liquor (Spirits)
Egypt	400	or	50	or	250	1
Jordan	200	or	25	or	200	1*
Lebanon	500	or	25	or	200	1

* open bottle only; non Jordanians only

A customs declaration is compulsory in certain Arab countries. You must list all currency, jewellery and mechanical or electrical appliances you're bringing in (cameras, radios, etc.). One copy of this form must be given to the customs officer. You'll keep the other which will be submitted to customs upon your departure. The above items, if personal effects, are duty-free; all the governments want to prevent is their being sold or exchanged by tourists.

I've nothing to declare.	ليس عندى شيء أعلن عنه .	**læysæ indi shæy' oolin 'ænho**
I've...	عندى ...	**indi**
a carton of cigarettes	خرطوشة سجاير	**khartūshit sægæyir**
a bottle of whisky	زجاجة وسكى	**zogægit wiski**
a bottle of wine	زجاجة نبيذ	**zogægit nibīt**
Must I pay on this?	هل يجب أن أدفع عن هذا ؟	**hæl yægib æn' ædfæ æn hæzæ**

How much?	كم ؟	kæm
It's for my personal use/It's not new.	انها لاستعمالى الشخصى / انها مستعملة .	**in**næhæ **lis**sti'mǣli **æsh**shakhsi/**in**næhæ mos**ta**'malæ

من فضلك افتح هذه الشنطة.	Please open this bag.
يجب أن تدفع جمرك عن هذا .	You'll have to pay duty on this.
من فضلك ادفع فى المكتب الموجود هناك .	Please pay at the office over there.
هل عندك أمتعة أخرى ؟	Have you any more luggage?

Changing money

Travellers aren't allowed to bring Egyptian pounds into Egypt, so don't try to change your money before leaving. You'll have to fill in a form stating how much money you have in cash and traveller's cheques. Keep the copy of this form, for you'll have to present it when you leave, along with each receipt you receive from a bank when you change money during your stay.

You'll be able to change money at a bank at any arrival point.

I want to change some...	أريد تحويل ...	o**rīd** tæḥ**wīl**
traveller's cheques	شيكات سياحية	**shi**kǣt siyǣ**ḥiy**yæ
dollars	دولارات	**do**larāt
pounds	جنيهات	**go**næyhǣt
Where's the nearest bank?	أين أقرب بنك ؟	æynæ **ak**rab bænk o**rīd** tæḥ**wīl**
What's the exchange rate?	ما سعر التحويل ؟	mǣ si'r il tæḥ**wīl**

Baggage—Porters

Porter!	شيال [عتال] !	shæyyæl [ættæl]
Can you help me with my luggage?	من فضلك ساعدنى فى حمل الحقائب !	min fadlak sæ'idni fi ḥæml il ḥæka'ib
That's mine.	هذه لى .	hæzihi li
The big/small/blue/brown/plaid one.	الكبيرة / الصغيرة / الزرقاء / البنى / المربعات.	æl kæbira/æl sagira/æl zærkā'/æl bonni/æl morabba'æt
There's one piece missing.	ناقص قطعة .	nākis kit'a
Take these bags to the...	خذ هذه الحقائب الى ...	khodd hæzihi il ḥakā'ib ilæ
taxi	التاكسى	æl tæksi
bus	الأوتوبيس	æl 'otobis
left-luggage office	الأمانات	æl 'æmænæt
How much is that?	بكم هذا ؟	bikæm hæzæ
Get me a taxi, please.	اطلب لى تاكسى من فضلك	otlob li tæksi min fadlak

Note: Porters' rates vary from one country to another. Have some small change ready. (For tipping, see inside back-cover.)

Directions

How do I get to...?	كيف أصل الى ... ؟	kæyfæ asil ilæ
Is there a bus into town?	هل يوجد أوتوبيس للبلد ؟	hæl yūgæd otobis lil bælæd
Where can I get a taxi?	أين أجد تاكسى ؟	æynæ 'ægid tæksi
Where can I rent a car?	أين يمكن تأجير سيارة ؟	æynæ yomkin tæ'gir sæyyāra

FOR NUMBERS, see page 175

Car rental

Car rental agencies operate in most larger centers and rates are usually attractive. You will also be able to hire chauffeur-driven cars through agencies located at most airpots as well as in major cities. It's highly likely that someone at the car-rental agency will speak English, but if nobody does, try one of the following:

I'd like to rent...	أريد تأجير ...	orīd tæ'gir
a small car	سيارة صغيرة	sæyyāra sagīra
a large car	سيارة كبيرة	sæyyāra kæbīra
a sports car	سيارة سبور	sæyyāra spōr
I'd like it...	أريدها ...	orīdohæ
for a day/for 4 days	لمدة يوم / لمدة أربعة أيام	limoddit yōm/limoddit 4 æyyæm
for a week/for 2 weeks	لمدة أسبوع / لمدة أسبوعين	limoddit osbū/limoddit osbu'ēn
I'd like to hire a chauffeur-driven car.	أريد تأجير سيارة بسائق [رميس] .	orīd tæ'gir sæyyāra bisǣ'ik (ramis)
What's the charge per day?	كم الثمن ليوم ؟	kæm il tæmæn liyōm
What's the charge per week?	كم الثمن لأسبوع ؟	kæm il tæmæn li 'osbū
Does that include mileage?	هل هذا يشمل العداد ؟	hæl hǣzæ yæshmæl il 'æddǣd
Does that include the services of a chauffeur?	هل هذا يشمل السائق ؟	hæl hǣzæ yæshmæl il sǣ'ik
Is petrol (gasoline) included?	هل هذا يشمل البنزين ؟	hæl hǣzæ yæshmæl il bænzin
Does that include full insurance?	هل هذا يشمل التأمين الشامل ؟	hæl hǣzæ yæshmæl il tæ'min il shǣmil
What's the deposit?	كم التأمين ؟	kæm il tæ'min
I have a credit card.	عندى بطاقة رصيد مصرفى .	indī bitākit rasīd masrafi

* see grammar

FOR DRIVING LICENCE, see page 145

Taxi

All taxis have meters, but you might ask the approximate fare beforehand. Taxi drivers expect to be tipped.

In addition to taxis, you'll find a collective-taxi service (sær**vis**) in Lebanon. This is a type of group taxi which follows a fixed route, picking up and letting passengers off along the way. Each pays the same fare and can get on or off anywhere he wishes along the route. This is a very popular means of transportation within cities as well as for inter-urban trips. Collective taxis are cheap, costing scarcely more than the bus.

Where can I get a taxi?	أين أجد تاكسى ؟	æynæ ægid **tæ**ksi
Get me a taxi, please.	أطلب لى تاكسى من فضلك .	**ot**lob li **tæ**ksi min **fad**lak
What's the fare to...?	كم الثمن الى ... ؟	kæm il**tæ**mæn **ilæ̈**
How far is it to...?	ما المسافة الى ... ؟	mæ̈ æl mæ**sæ̈**fæ **ilæ̈**
Take me to...	خذنى الى ...	**khod**ni ilæ̈
this address/the town centre/the ... hotel	هذا العنوان/ وسط البلد/ فندق ...	**hæ̈**zæl 'in**wæ̈n**/**wa**sat il bælæd/**fon**dok
Turn left/right at the next corner.	الى الشمال / اليمين فى الشارع القادم .	ilæ̈ æsh**shi**mæ̈l/æl yæmin fil **shæ̈**ri' æl **kā**dim
Go straight ahead.	استمر الى الامام .	istæ**mirr** ilæl æ**mæ̈**m
Stop here, please.	قف هنا من فضلك .	kiff **ho**næ̈ min **fad**lak
I'm in a hurry.	أنا مستعجل .	æ**næ̈** mis**ta**'gil
Could you drive more slowly?	من فضلك سق على مهلك .	min **fad**lak sūk æ**læ̈** **mæh**læk
Could you help to carry my bags?	من فضلك ساعدنى فى حمل شنطى .	min **fad**lak sæ̈'**id**ni fi ḥæml **sho**nati

FOR TIPPING, see inside back-cover

Hotel—Other accommodation

Early reservation (and confirmation) is essential in most major tourist centres during the high season. You may have to pay a supplementary charge on Islamic high holidays.

فندق (fondok)	Hotel. There's no official classification of hotels in the Middle East, but you'll find those of the highest international standards as well as others which seem to have no standards at all! You'd be well advised to choose a hotel with care, thus avoiding any unpleasant surprise. Your travel agent or the local tourist office usually has a list of hotels in three or more price categories.
بنسيون (pænsyōn)	Boarding house. Generally occupying a floor of an apartment block, boarding houses are found in most towns. Prices are reasonable, and service is good. If you plan to stay a week or so, ask the manager for a reduction.
شقق مفروشة (shokæk mæfrūshæ)	Furnished flats (apartments). Found particularly in Cairo and Beirut, such accommodation is cheap and practical for longer stays (several weeks).
بيت شباب (bēt shæbæb)	Youth hostel. These are found in most Middle Eastern countries. Inquire at the local tourist office or at the Youth Hostels Association in your own country before leaving home.

In this section, we're mainly concerned with the smaller and medium-class hotels. You'll have no language difficulties in the luxury and first-class hotels where most of the staff can speak English.

In the next few pages we consider your basic requirements, step by step, from arrival to departure. You need not read all of it, just turn to the situation that applies.

Checking in—Reception

My name is...	اسمى ...	ismi
I have a reservation.	عندى حجز .	indi ḥægz
We've reserved 2 rooms, a single and a double.*	حجزنا غرفتين . غرفة لشخص وغرفة لشخصين .	ḥægæznæ gorfatēn. gorfa lishakhs wæ gorfa lishakhsēn
Here's the confirmation.	هذا تأكيد الحجز .	hæzæ tæ'kid æl ḥægz
I'd like a...	أريد ...	orid
single room	غرفة لشخص	gorfa lishakhs
double room	غرفة لشخصين	gorfa lishakhsēn
suite	جناح	gænæh
room with twin beds	غرفة بسريرين	gorfa bisirīrēn
room with a bath	غرفة لها حمام	gorfa læhæ ḥæmmæm
room with a shower	غرفة لها دوش	gorfa læhæ dosh
room with a balcony	غرفة لها بلكونة	gorfa læhæ bælkōnæ
room with a view	غرفة بها منظر جميل	gorfa bihæ manzar gæmil
We'd like a room...	نريد غرفة ...	norid gorfa
in the front	فى الأمام	fil æmæm
at the back	فى الخلف	fil khælf
facing the sea	تطل على البحر	totill 'ælæl baḥr
facing the gardens	تطل على الحديقة	totill 'ælæl ḥædika

* see grammar

FOR NUMBERS, see page 175

It must be quiet.	لا بد أن تكون هادئة .	læ**bodd** æn tæ**kūn** hæ**di'æ**
Is there...?	هل يوجد ... ؟	hæll **yū**gæd
air conditioning	تكييف هواء	tæ**kyif** hæ**wæ**
heating	تدفئة	tæd**fi'**æ
a radio/television in the room	راديو / تليفزيون فى الغرفة	**rad**yo/tili**visyōn** fil **gorfa**
a laundry	غسيل ومكوة	gæ**sil** wæ **mæk**wæ
room service	خدمة فى الغرفة	**khid**mæ fil **gorfa**
hot water	ماء ساخن	**mæ'** sæ**khin**
running water	ماء جارى	**mæ'** gæ**ri**
a private toilet	تواليت خاص	twæ**litt** khās

How much?

What's the price...?	كم الثمن ... ؟	kæm æl **tæ**mæn
per night	لمدة يوم	li**mod**dit yōm
per week	لمدة أسبوع	li**mod**dit **os**bū
for bed and breakfast	للنوم والفطار	lil**nōm** wæl fi**tār**
excluding meals	بدون وجبات	bi**dūn** wæg**bæt**
for full board	للاقامة الكاملة	lil i**kā**mæ æl **kæ**milæ
for half board	لنصف الاقامة	li**nisf** æl 'i**kā**mæ
Does that include meals/service?	هل هذا يشمل الوجبات / الخدمة ؟	hæl **hæ**zæ **yæsh**mæl æl **wæg**bæt/æl **khid**mæ
Is there any reduction for children?	هل يوجد تخفيض للاطفال ؟	hæl **yū**gæd **takh**fid lil **at**fāl
Do you charge for the baby?	هل تحاسب على الطفل ؟	hæl to**ḥæ**sib 'ælæl tifl
That's too expensive.	هذا غالى جداً .	**hæ**zæ **gæ**li **gid**dæn
Haven't you anything cheaper?	هل عندك شيء أرخص ؟	hæl **in**dæk shē' **ar**khass

FOR NUMBERS, see page 175

How long?

We'll be staying...	سنبقى ...	sænæbkā
overnight only	الليلة فقط	æl lēlæ fakatt
a few days	بضعة أيام	bid'at ǣyyǣm
a week (at least)	أسبوع (على الأقل)	osbū (ælæl akall)
I don't know yet.	لا أعرف بعد .	lǣ āraf bæ'd

Decision

May I see the room?	أريد أن أرى الغرفة من فضلك .	orīdænaralgorfaminfadlak
No, I don't like it.	لا . انها لا تعجبنى .	lǣ. innæhǣ lǣ to'gibni
It's too...	انها . . . جداً .	innæhǣ...giddæn
cold/hot	باردة / ساخنة	bǣridæ/sǣkhinæ
dark/small	ضلمة / صغيرة	dalma/sagīræ
noisy	دوشه	dæwshæ
I asked for a room with a bath.	طلبت غرفة بحمام .	talabt gorfa biḥæmmǣm
Have you anything...?	هل عندك شيء ... ؟	hæl indæk shē'
better/bigger	أحسن / أكبر	æḥsæn/akbar
cheaper/quieter	أرخص / أهدأ	arkhass/æhdæ'
That's fine. I'll take it.	كويس . سآخذها .	kwæyyis. sæ'ǣkhozhæ

Bills

Provided an extra room isn't required, there's often a reduction of 50 per cent in luxury and first-class hotels for children up to the age of six, and 30 per cent for 6–12 year-olds. Enquire about a similar arrangement at smaller hotels.

A service charge is normally included in the bill, but you can ask:

Is service included?	هل الخدمة محسوبة ؟	hæl æl khidmæ mæḥsūbæ

FOR TIPPING, see back-cover

Registration

On arrival at a hotel or boarding house you'll be asked to fill in a registration form. It asks your name, home address, passport number and further destination. It's almost certain to carry an English translation. If it doesn't, ask the desk clerk:

What does this mean?	ما معنى هذا ؟	mǣ mææntæ hǣzæ

The desk clerk will probably ask you for your passport. He may want to keep it for a while, even overnight. Don't worry—you'll get it back. The desk clerk may want to ask you the following questions:

أريد أن أرى الباسبور من فضلك .	May I see your passport?
من فضلك املأ هذه الاستمارة .	Would you mind filling in this registration form?
من فضلك وقّـع هنا .	Sign here, please.
ما طول مدة اقامتك ؟	How long will you be staying?

What's my room number?	ما نمرة غرفتى ؟	mǣ **nim**rit gorfatī
Will you have our bags sent up?	من فضلك ارسل الحقائب فوق .	min **fad**lak **ir**sil il ḥakā'ib fōk
I'd like to leave this in your safe.	أريد أن أترك هذا فى الخزنة .	o**rīd** æn ætrok **hǣ**zæ fil **khæz**næ

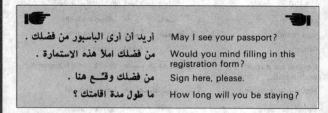

Service, please

Apart from maids, hotel staff in the Middle East is generally only composed of men.

maid	خادمة الغرفة	khǣ**di**mæt æl **gor**fæ
manager	المدير	æl **mo**dir
room service	الخدمة فى الغرفة	æl **khid**mæ fil **gor**fæ
switchboard operator	عامل التليفون	ǣmil il **ti**lifōn

If you want to call the members of the staff, say: Please (min **fad**lak)!

General requirements

Please ask the maid to come up.	من فضلك اطلب من خادمة الغرفة أن تصعد .	min **fad**lak **ot**lob min khǣ**di**mæt æl **gor**fæ æn **tas**'ad
Who is it?	مين ؟	min
Just a minute.	لحظة واحدة !	**la**ḥza **wæḥ**dæ
Come in!	أدخل !	**od**kholl
Is there a bath on this floor?	هل يوجد حمام فى هذا الطابق ؟	hæl **yū**gæd ḥæm**mǣm** fi **hǣ**zæl **tā**bik
Please send up...	من فضلك ارسل لنا ...	min **fad**lak **ir**sil **læ**nǣ
two coffees/a sandwich	فنجالين قهوة / سسندوتش	fingæ**lēn æh**wæ/ sændæ**witsh**
a bottle of mineral water	زجاجة مياه معدنية	zo**gǣ**git mi**yǣ**h mæ'dæ**niy**yæ
Can we have breakfast in our room?	هل يمكن الافطار فى غرفتنا؟	hæl **yom**kin æl **'if**tār fi gor**fa**tinǣ
May I have a/an/some...?	من فضلك أريد ...	min **fad**lak o**rīd**
ashtray	طفاية سجاير	taf**fā**yit sæ**gǣ**yir
bath towel	فوطة حمام	**fū**tit hæm**mǣm**

extra blanket	بطانية زيادة	battaniyya ziyǣdæ
envelopes	ظروف	zorūf
(more) hangers	علاقات (زيادة)	ællǣkāt (ziyǣdæ)
hot-water bottle	قربة ماء ساخن	irbit mæ' sǣkhin
ice cubes	قطع ثلج	kita' tælg
needle and thread	ابرة وخيط	ibræ wæ khēt
extra pillow	مخدة زيادة	mækhæddæ ziyǣdæ
reading-lamp	لمبة للقراءة	lamba lil kirā'a
soap	صابون	sabūn
writing-paper	ورق للكتابة	wæræ' lil kitǣbæ
Where's the...?	أين يوجد ... ؟	æynæ yūgæd
bar	البار	æl bār
barber's	حلاق	ḥællāk
bathroom	الحمام	æl ḥæmmǣm
beauty salon	صالون التجميل	salōn æl tægmil
dining room	صالة الطعام	sālit æl ta'ām
restaurant	المطعم	æl mat'am
television room	صالة التليفزيون	sālit æl tilivisyōn
toilet	التواليت	æl twælitt

Breakfast

In the Middle East, breakfast consists of *fool* (black beans), white cheese, *halava* (a sugary confection) and *falafel* (fried balls of ground *fool*). If this doesn't suit your palate, most top-class hotels serve continental or American breakfasts.

I'll have a/an/some...	أريد . . .	orīd
eggs	بيض	bēd
boiled egg	بيضة مسلوقة	bēda mæslu'æ
soft/medium/hard	نصف سواء/متوسط/ جـامد	nisf siwæ/motæwassit/ gǣmid
fried egg	بيضة مقلية	bēda makliyya

fruit juice	عصير فاكهة	assīr fǣkihæ
grapefruit/orange	جريب فروت/برتقال	grēp frūt/bortokāl
pineapple/tomato	أناناس/طماطم	ænænǣs/tamātim
omelet	عجة	’igga
May I have some...?	أريد ... من فضلك	orīd...min fadlak
bread/toast	خبز / توست	khobz/tost
hot/cold milk	لبن ساخن / لبن بارد	læbæn sǣkhin/ læbæn bǣrid
cream/sugar	كريم / سكر	krēm/sokkar
more butter	زبد زيادة	zibdæ ziyǣdæ
salt/pepper	ملح / فلفل	mælḥ/filfil
coffee/tea	قهوة / شاى	æhwæ/shǣy
hot chocolate	شكولاتة ساخنة	shokolāta sokhnæ
lemon/honey	ليمون / عسل	læmūn/æsæl
jam/marmalade	مربى / مربى برتقال	marabba/marabbit bortokāl
Could you bring me a...	من فضلك احضرلى ...	min fadlak iḥdir lī
plate	صحن	sahn
glass	كباية	kobbǣyæ
cup	فنجان	fingǣn
knife	سكينة	sikkīnæ
fork	شوكة	shōkæ
spoon	ملعقة	mil’aka

Difficulties

The ... doesn't work.	ال ... لا يعمل .	il...lǣ yæ’mæl
air conditioner	تكييف الهواء	tækyīf hæwǣ
fan	مروحة	marwaḥa
light	نور	nūr
tap	صنبور [حنفية]	sonbūr [ḥænæfiyyæ]
toilet	تواليت	twælitt

FOR EATING OUT, see pages 38–64

The wash basin is blocked.	الحوض مسدود .	æl ḥōd mæs**dūd**
The window is jammed.	الشباك من الصعب فتحه.	æl shib**bǣk** min æl **saab** fæt**ḥo**
The blind is stuck.	الغمامات لا تعمل .	æl gæmæ**mǣt** læ **tæ**æmæl
These aren't my shoes.	هذا ليس حذائى .	**hǣ**zæ **læy**sæ ḥi**zǣ**'i
This isn't my laundry.	هذا ليس غسيلى .	**hǣ**zæ **læy**sæ gæ**sīli**
There's no hot water.	لا يوجد ماء ساخن .	lǣ **yū**gæd mǣ' **sǣ**khin
I've lost my watch.	ساعتى ضاعت .	sǣ'æti dā'**it**
I've left my key in my room.	لقد تركت المفتاح فى غرفتى .	ta**rakt** æl **mof**tǣḥ fi **gor**fati
The bulb is burnt out.	لمبة النور محروقة .	lam**bit** æl nūr mæḥ**rū**ka
The ... is broken.	الـ ... مكسور .	æl ... **mak**sūr
lamp	مصباح	**mis**bāḥ
plug	كبس	kobs
shutter/window shade	شيش / غمامات	shīsh/gæm**mæ**mǣt
switch	مفتاح النور	**mof**tǣḥ æl nūr
Can you get it fixed?	هل يمكن اصلاحها ؟	hæl **yom**kin islā**ḥi**hǣ

Telephone—Mail—Callers

Can you get me Cairo 123456?	أريد الاتصال بالقاهرة رقم ١٢٣٤٥٦ .	o**rīd** æl '**it**tisāl bil kā**hi**ra **ra**kam 12 34 56
Did anyone telephone me?	هل اتصل بى أحد تليفونيا؟	hæl it**ta**sala bī 'æḥæd tilifō**niy**yæn
Is there any mail for me?	هل توجد خطابات لى؟	hæl **tū**gæd khita**bǣt** li
Have you any stamps?	هل عندك طوابع بريد ؟	hæl **æn**dæk ta**wā**bi' bæ**rīd**
Would you please mail this for me?	هل يمكنك ارسال هذا بالبريد ؟	hæl yom**ki**næk ir**sǣl** **hǣ**za bil bæ**rīd**
Are there any messages for me?	هل توجد رسالة لى؟	hæl **tū**gæd ri**sǣ**læ li

FOR POST OFFICE AND TELEPHONE, see page 137

HOTEL SERVICE

Checking out

May I have my bill, please? Room 398.	أريد فاتورة حسابى من فضلك غرفة رقم ٣٩٨.	orīd fatūrit ḥisæbi min fadlak. gorfæ rakam 398
I'm leaving early tomorrow.	سأرحل مبكراً صباح الغد .	sæ'arḥal mobækkiran sabāḥ æl gædd
Please have my bill ready.	من فضلك جهز لى الفاتورة.	min fadlak gæhhizli æl fatūra
We'll be checking out around noon.	سنرحل حوالى الظهر .	sænarḥal ḥawæli æl zohr
I must leave at once.	لا بد أن أرحل فوراً .	læbodd æn arḥal fawran
Does this include service?	هل هذا يشمل الخدمة ؟	hæl hæzæ yæshmæl æl khidmæ
Is everything included?	هل كل شيء محسوب ؟	hæl koll shē' mæḥsūb
You've made a mistake in this bill, I think.	أظن أنك أخطات فى حساب هذه الفاتورة .	azonn 'ænnækæ akhta't fi ḥisæb hæzihi æl fatūra
Can you get us a taxi?	من فضلك اطلب لنا تاكسى .	min fadlak otlob lænæ tæksi
When's the next... to Cairo?	متى موعد ... القادم الى القاهرة ؟	mætæ maw'id æl..æl kādim ilæ ælkāhira
bus/train/plane	الأوتوبيس / القطار / الطائرة	æl 'otobīs/æl kitār/ æl tā'ira
Would you send someone to bring down our baggage?	من فضلك ارسل أحداً لانزال الحقائب .	min fadlak irsil 'æḥædæn li'inzæl æl ḥakā'ib
We're in a great hurry.	اننا فى غاية الاستعجال .	innænæ fi gāyæt æl 'isti'gæl
Here's the forwarding address. You have my home address.	هذا هو عنواننا القادم . عندك عنوان منزلى .	hæzæ howæ inwænonæ æl kādim. indæk innwæn mænzili
It's been a very enjoyable stay.	كانت الاقامة ممتعة جداً .	kænæt æl 'ikāma momti'æ giddæn

FOR TAXI, see page 27

Eating out

There are many types of places where you can eat and drink in the Arab countries.

مطعم (**mat**'am)	A restaurant; there's often a set menu, especially in European ones.
حـاتى (**ḥæ**ti)	A restaurant specializing in charcoal-grilled lamb.
مطعم لحم مشوى (**mat**'am laḥm **mæsh**wi)	Same as the above, only the name is different in Lebanon.
مطعم حمـام (**mat**'am ḥæ**mǣm**)	A restaurant specializing in pigeon or squab
مطعم سمك (**mat**'am **sæ**mæk)	Fish and seafood restaurant.
فول وفـلافل (fūl wæ fæ**lǣ**fil)	A snack-bar; this is a popular type of eating place serving *fool* (black-bean dish) and *falafel* (small balls of ground black beans, fried and served with a choice of spices). *Fool* and *falafel* may also be a filling for sandwiches.
كافيتريـا (kæfi**tir**yæ)	A snack-bar; you may have to eat standing up.
محـل عصير (mæ**ḥæl** 'asīr)	Fruit-juice bar (sometimes it's a drive-in); features fresh fruit juice. Often you can get *shawerma*—thin slices of spitroasted lamb—and sandwiches.
صالون شاى (sa**lōn** shǣy)	A coffee shop; it's often a part of a pastry shop.
حلويـات شامى (ḥælæwiy**yǣt sh**ǣmi)	A Lebanese or Syrian pastry shop.
ملهى ليـلى (**mæl**hæ **læ**yli)	Night-club (cabaret); dinner and a show; in Egypt all the shows feature the famed belly dancers whom you won't want to miss.

كاس عرق ومازة (kǣs ʻarak wæ mǣzæ) A restaurant in Lebanon which serves salads and appetizers among other local dishes. This type of restaurant traditionally serves *arak*, an aniseed liqueur and the national drink, as beverage.

There are also neighbourhood restaurants, many of which specialize in a particular dish such as *kosharee* (rice, lentils and hot sauce), *kebda wa mokh* (liver and brains) or *fiseekh* (dried fish).

Eating habits

In this section we're primarily concerned with restaurants—and with lunch and dinner. We assume that you've already had breakfast at your hotel.

In the Arab countries, meals are generally eaten later than at home—both privately and in restaurants.

غذاء (gædæ) Lunch is generally served from 1 to 3 p.m.

عشاء (ʻæshæ) Dinner is served from 8 to 11 p.m. In night-clubs you'll be able to dine even after midnight.

If you feel hungry at an unusual hour, you'll always be able to find a restaurant or a snack-bar serving warm dishes or snacks at any time of the day or night.

Most large restaurants in major cities specialize in European dishes, especially French and Italian, rather than Middle Eastern cuisine. But you'll usually find some Middle Eastern dishes on the menu. Unless you're specifically looking for European food, avoid the big restaurants and go to local eating places.

In summer many restaurants as well as night-clubs move outdoors to take advantage of the fine weather.

FOR BREAKFAST, see page 34

What is Ramadan?

The month of Ramadan is one of Islam's holy periods. As it's a lunar month, it has no regular corresponding date in the calendar year. It's observed by Moslems in all Arab countries by fasting and by refraining from drinking and smoking from sunrise to sunset. This religious rite is a way of showing one's obedience to God and of strengthening social relations.

The main meal of the day which is taken at sunset is called *iftar*. It usually starts with a hot soup, then goes on with *fool* and eggs, generally mixed together, and the rest of the meal is a normal one, followed by oriental sweets. The characteristic drink of this month (non-alcoholic, of course) is *kamar-eldin*. It's made of a stewed apricot purée which is served fresh. Just try it and you'll surely ask for more.

Iftar provides the opportunity to meet friends and relatives; it's also a time of charity when beggars, who knock at the door at this special period of the year, will be given food. After *iftar*, people usually listen to music and to readings from the Koran on the radio and go to the mosque. Restaurants and cafés stay open all night and are well patronized. Later on, at about 1 or 2 a.m., you take your second meal of the "day", called *sohur*, which helps the Moslem to endure the long hours of fasting to come.

During Ramadan, public places are open all night and the streets are brightly illuminated. Nevertheless, one shouldn't forget that the month of Ramadan is first and foremost a religious month.

But don't worry: non-Moslem visitors aren't expected to fast. You'll find eating places open specially for you.

Hungry

I'm hungry/I'm thirsty.	أنا جوعان / أنا عطشان .	'ænæ gæ'**ǣn**/'ænǣ 'atshān
Can you recommend a good (and inexpensive) restaurant?	من فضلك انصحنى بمطعم جيد (ورخيص) .	min **fad**lak 'insaḥni bimat'am **gæ**yyid (wæ rakhīs)
I'd like to reserve a table for 4.	أريـد أن أحجز ترابيـزة [طاولة] لـ ٤ .	orīd æn 'æḥgiz tara**bē**za [**taw**la] li 4
We'll come at 8.	سنأتى الساعة ٨ .	sænæ'ti æl **sǣ**æ 8

Asking and ordering

Could we have a...?	من فضلك نريد ...	min **fad**lak no**rīd**
table in the corner	ترابيزة [طاولة] منعزلة	tara**bē**za [**taw**la] mon'æzilæ
table by the window	ترابيزة [طاولة] بجانب الشباك	tara**bē**za [**taw**la] bi**gǣ**nib æl shib**bǣk**
table outside	ترابيزة [طاولة] فى الخـارج	tara**bē**za [**taw**la] fil **khǣ**rig
What's the price of the set menu?	ما هو ثمن الوجبة ؟	mǣ **how**æ **tæ**mæn æl **wæg**bæ
Is service included?	هل الخدمة محسوبة ؟	hæl æl **khid**mæ mæḥ**sū**bæ
Could we have a(n) ... please?	من فضلك نريد ...	min **fad**lak no**rīd**
ashtray	طفاية سجاير [منفضة]	taf**fā**yit sæ**gǣ**yir [**man**fada]
finger bowl	كاس ماء لغسل الأصابع	kǣs **may**ya li**gæsl** æl'asābi'
fork	شوكـة	**shō**kæ
glass	كبـاية	kob**bǣ**yæ
knife	سكينـة	sik**kī**næ
plate	صحن	saḥn
serviette (napkin)	فوطـة	**fū**ta
spoon	ملعقـة	mal'aka
tablecloth	مفرش سفرة	**maf**rash **sof**ra
toothpick	مسلكـة أسنان	mæslækit 'æs**nǣn**

FOR COMPLAINTS, see page 59

I'd like a/an/some...	أريد ...	orīd
beer	بيرة	bīræ
bread	عيش [خبز]	'ēsh [khobz]
butter	زبدة	zibdæ
cheese	جبنة	gibnæ
chips (french fries)	شيبس	ships
coffee	قهوة	'æhwæ
fish	سمك	sæmæk
fowl	دجاج	dægǣg
fruit	فاكهة	fækhæ
ice-cream	جلاس [بوظة]	glǣs [būza]
lemon	ليمون [حامض]	læymūn [ḥāmid]
lettuce	خس	khass
meat	لحم	læḥm
milk	لبن حليب	læbæn ḥælīb
mineral water	مياه معدنية	mayya mæ'dæniyyæ
mustard	مستردة [خردل]	mostarda [khærdæl]
noodles	مكرونة شريط	makarōna shirīt
olive oil	زيت زيتون	zēt zætūn
pepper	فلفل [بهار]	filfil [bohār]
potatoes	بطاطس	batātis
rice	رز	roz
rolls	خبز سندوتش	khobz sændæwitsh
salad	صلطة	salata
salt	ملح	mælḥ
sandwich	سندوتش	sændæwitsh
soup	شوربة	shorba
sugar	سكر	sokkar
tea	شاى	shǣy
vegetables	خضار	khodār
vinegar	خل	khæl
(iced) water	مياه (مثلجة)	mayya (mitælligæ)
wine	نبيذ	nibīt

What's on the menu

Our menu is presented according to courses. Under each heading you'll find an alphabetical list of dishes in Arabic with their English equivalents. This list—which includes everyday and special dishes—will enable you to make the most of an Arabic menu.

Here's our guide to good eating and drinking. Turn to the course you want to start with.

Arab cooking is in many ways typical of what you'll find throughout the Mediterranean. Many popular dishes of Egypt, for example, have been inherited from the Turks or the Circassians, a Moslem people who emigrated from Russia in the last century. Much emphasis is placed on grilling or slowly braising vegetable or meat stews.

Appetizers—Starters

It's customary in Arab countries to serve a variety of appetizers and salads with the aperitif. These are called the *mezza*. This consists of numerous small plates of hors d'œuvre. Lebanon is especially noted for the diversity and tastiness of its *mezza*. A complete one consists of about 40 different appetizers. We don't have room to name them all, but here's a sampling of some popular ones.

I'd like an appetizer.	أريد فاتح شهية من فضلك .	orīd fǣtiḥ shæhiyyæ min fadlak

أنشوجة	'ænshūgæ	anchovies
اسبرجس	'asparagas	asparagus tips
خرشوف [أرضى شوكى]	kharshūf ['ardī shōkī]	artichokes
بيض	bēd	eggs
بيض بالمايونيز	bēd bil mæyonēz	egg salad
رنجة	ringæ	herring
رنجة مملحة	ringæ momællæḥæ	salted-herring fillets
زيتون	zætūn	olives
مخللات [كبيس]	mikhællilǣt [kæbīs]	pickles (pickled vegetables)
كبد الوز	kæbid ælwiz	goose-liver pâté
كبد دجاج	kæbid dægǣg	chopped chicken liver
عصير فاكهة	'asīr fækhæ	fruit juice
شمام	shæmmǣm	melon
سلامى	sælǣmi	salami
سجق [مقانق]	sogo' [mæ'ǣnik]	sausages
سردين	særdīn	sardines
كركند	karakænd	lobster
باتيه [فواجرا]	pætēh [fwagrā]	pâté
جندفلى [محار]	gændoflī [maḥḥār]	oysters
كافيار	kavyār	caviar

Arabic specialities

باذنجان مخلل (bitingæn mikhællil)	aubergine (eggplant) stuffed with herbs, garlic and spices.
ورق عنب محشي (wæræ' 'inæb mæḥshi)	grape leaves stuffed with rice and minced meat; may be served cold or hot.
طحينة (tiḥīna)	a paste made with ground sesame seeds and spices; particularly good with fish.
بابا غنوج (babagænnūg)	*tehina* to which mashed aubergine (eggplant) is added.
حمص بطحينة (ḥommos bitḥīna)	a spicy paste made with ground chick-peas, *tehina* and spices.
جبنة بيضاء بالطماطم (gibnæ bēda bil tamātim)	white cheese served with tomatoes, onion, parsley, oil and lemon; sometimes a hot sauce is added.
بطارخ (batārikh)	"Egyptian caviar", red fish roe
عجة ('iggæ)	omelet, made of onions, parsley and green pepper; baked.

Salads

What salads do you have?	ما أصناف الصلاطة عندكم ؟	mæ 'asnāf ælsalata ændokom

صلاطة خيار وطماطم [بندورة]	salatit khiyār wæ tamātim [banadūra]	cucumber and tomato salad
صلاطة بطاطس	salatit batātis	potato salad
صلاطة كرفس	salatit karafs	celery salad
صلاطة خس	salatit khass	lettuce salad
صلاطة باذنجان	salatit bitingæn	aubergine (eggplant) salad
صلاطة بنجر [شمندر]	salatit bangar	beetroot salad
صلاطة جرجير	salatit gærgīr	watercress salad

Salad specialities

Can you recommend a local speciality?	من فضلك انصحني بأكلة محلية .	min **fad**lak 'in**saḥ**ni bi '**æk**læ mæḥæl**liy**yæ

لبن زبادي وخيار (læbæn zæ**bǣ**di wæ khi**yār**)	diced cucumbers with a dressing of yogurt, olive oil, garlic and mint leaves
صلاطة بلدي (**sa**lata **bæ**lædi)	salad of cucumbers, tomatoes, onions, watercress, parsley, green peppers, mint leaves (Egypt)
تبولة (tæb**bū**læ)	Lebanese salad, similar to the Egyptian one, but with cracked wheat and bread crumbs

Cheese

In Arab countries a lot of cheese is eaten, and it's eaten with the meal, not after the main course. Moreover, it's served most frequently with breakfast and supper. You'll also find it served under various guises as a part of the *mezza,* or appetizers.

جبنة بيضاء من لبن معيز (**gib**næ **bē**da min læbæn mi'**īz**)	white goat's milk cheese
جبنة مالحة (**gib**næ **mæl**ḥæ)	salted fresh-curd cheese
جبنة أريش (**gib**næ 'æ**rīsh**)	full, rich cheese, slightly salty
جبنة ريكوتا (**gib**næ ri**kot**ta)	a type of cottage cheese
مش (mesh)	well aged, very salty and sharp
لبنة (**læb**næ)	a fresh-curd cheese sprinkled with olive oil

EATING OUT

Soup

You'll find many different kinds of soup in the Middle East, among them many European and American favourites as well as regional specialities. Lentil soup is the most popular of the local soups.

I'd like some soup.	أريد شوربة من فضلك .	orīd **shor**ba min **fad**lak
What do you recommend?	بم تنصح ؟	bi**mæ tan**saḥ

شوربة عدس	**shor**bit 'æds	lentil soup
شوربة فراخ [دجاج]	**shor**bit fi**rækh**	chicken soup
شوربة لحم	**shor**bit læḥm	meat soup
شوربة باذلاء	**shor**bit bisillæ	pea soup
شوربة خضار	**shor**bit kho**dār**	vegetable soup
شوربة سمك	**shor**bit sæmæk	fish soup
شوربة بصل	**shor**bit **ba**sal	onion soup
شوربة طماطم [بندورة]	**shor**bit tamātim [bana**dū**ra]	tomato soup
شوربة شعرية	**shor**bit shi'**riy**yæ	noodle soup
شوربة عدس بحامض	**shor**bit 'æds bi**ḥā**mid	lentil and lemon soup (Lebanon)

Fish and seafood

Alexandria and Beirut are especially good places to sample fish and seafood, and you'll want to try the grilled shrimps. Aboukir is a fishing village near Alexandria where you can taste the catch fresh from the Mediterranean. If you're lucky, a fisherman may suggest grilling a fish for you right at the seaside. In Cairo, you're likely to eat fish from the Nile. Very often you'll find there is a fishmonger's attached to the restaurant. Consequently you can be sure of having fresh fish and can even pick the one you want for dinner.

I'd like some fish.	أريد سمكاً من فضلك .	orīd **sæ**mæk min **fad**lak
What kinds of seafood do you have?	أى أصناف السمك عندكم ؟	'æyy 'as**nāf** æl **sæ**mæk 'æn**do**kom

In addition to a lot of exotic local fish, here are the names of a few more common varieties:

أنشوجة	æn**shū**gæ	anchovies
استاكوزا [كركند]	istæ**kō**zæ [kæræ**kænd**]	lobster
جمبرى [قرادس]	gæm**bæ**ri ['ær**ǣ**dis]	shrimp
جندفلى [محار]	gæn**do**fli [maḥ**ḥār**]	oysters
كابوريا	kæ**bor**yæ	crab
سردين	sær**dīn**	sardines
تونة	**tū**næ	tunny (tuna)
سمك موسى	sæmæk **mū**sæ	sole

Some of the ways you may want your fish served:

baked	فى الفرن	fil forn
cured	مملح	mo**mæl**læḥ
fried	مقلى	**mæ**'li
grilled	مشوى	**mæsh**wi
marinated	متبَّل	mo**tæb**bæl
poached	مسلوق	mæs**lū**'
smoked	مدخن	mo**dækh**khæn
steamed	بالبخار	bil bo**khār**

كباب سمك (kæ**bǣb** sæmæk)	chunks of fish, stewed and charcoal grilled with pieces of tomatoes and green pepper
سمك صيادية (**sæ**mæk sayya**di**yyæ)	chunks of fish cooked in oil and served with rice flavoured with the fish cooking oil

Meat

Eating pork is forbidden according to Moslem dietary laws, therefore it's rarely found on a menu.

What kinds of meat do you have?	أى أصناف اللحم عندكم ؟	'ævy 'asnāf ællæḥm 'ændokom
I'd like some...	أريد لحم ...	orīd læḥm
beef/veal/lamb	بقرى/بتلو/ضانى	bæ'æri/bitillo/dāni

أوزى	'ūzi	baby lamb
ريش [كستليتة] ضانى	riyæsh [kostælētæ] dāni	lamb chops
لسان	lisæn	tongue
اسكالوب	'iskælop	scallop
جامبون – خنزير	zhæmbōn-khænzīr	ham
كوارع بتلو	kæwæri' bitillo	calf's trotters (feet)
لحم مفروم	læḥm mafrūm	minced meat
كستليتة	kostælētæ	cutlets
موزة	mōzæ	shank, knuckle
سجق [مقانق]	sogo' [mæ'ænik]	sausages
كستليتة بتلو [عجل]	kostælētæ bitillo ['igl]	veal chops
بفتيك	boftēk	beef steak
فخذ (ضانى)	fækhdæ (dāni)	leg (of lamb)
مخ	mokh	brains
كلاوى	kælæwi	kidneys
كتف	kitf	shoulder
روسبيف	rozbīf	roast beef
رأس [نيفة]	rās [nīfæ]	head
رقبة	ræ'æbæ	neck
فيلتو	filitto	fillet
صدر	sidr	breast
كبدة	kibdæ	liver
كفتة	koftæ	meatballs
كرشة	kirshæ	tripe

Arabic meat dishes

كبــاب (kæbææb)	spicy chunks of charcoal-grilled lamb
ريش (riyæsh)	spicy charcoal-grilled lamb chops
كفــتة (koftæ)	charcoal-grilled minced meatballs
شاورمــة (shawirmæ)	chunks of lamb roasted on a vertical spit from which thin slices are cut and served either in a bun or on a plate, usually with rice; a popular snack served from roadside stands
كبيبة [كبــة] (kobēbæ [kibbæ])	minced meat, cracked wheat, onion, baked in butter; it can be served raw *(kobeiba naya)*, baked *(kobeiba besseniyah)* or rolled into dumplings and served in goat's milk soup *(kobeiba labniyeh)* (Lebanon)
مقلــوبة (mæ'lūbæ)	meat and aubergine (eggplant) served with rice
فتــة (fættæ)	boiled mutton and rice mixed with bread crumbs and broth, served with vinegar and garlic
صفيحــة (sfiḥæ)	a pastry crust like pizza garnished with seasoned minced mutton (Lebanon)

barbecued	مشوى على الفحم	mæshwi 'ælæl fæḥm
fried	مقــلى	mæ'li
grilled	مشوى	mæshwi
roasted	رستــو	rosto
stewed	مسلــوق	mæslū'
stuffed	محشى	mæḥshi
underdone (rare)	قليــل السواء	kalīl ælsiwæ
medium	نصف سواء	nisf siwæ
well-done	مستــوى	mistiwi

Game and fowl

I'd like some game. . أريد طيــور orid toyūr

أرنب	'ærnæb	rabbit
بط	batt	duck
بط بــرّى	batt **bærri**	wild duck
حمـام	hæ**mǣm**	pigeon
ديك رومى [حبشى]	dik **rūmi** [ḥæbæsh]	turkey
سمان [سمــّن]	simm**ǣn** [**som**mon]	quail
فراخ [فراريج]	fir**ǣkh** [fr**ǣ**rizh]	chicken
ورك/صدر/كبدة	wirk/sidr/**kib**dæ	leg/breast/liver
فراخ [فراريج] مشوية	fir**ǣkh** [fr**ǣ**rizh] mæsh**wiy**yæ	roast chicken
وز	wizz	goose

Game and poultry dishes

فراخ شركسية
(fir**ǣkh** shærkæ**siy**yæ)
boiled chicken served with boiled rice and a sauce made of chopped walnuts, chili pepper and bread

فراخ بالخلطة
(fir**ǣkh** bil **khal**ta)
roast chicken served with rice mixed with nuts, chicken liver and giblets

كشك بالفراخ
(kishk bil fir**ǣkh**)
pieces of boiled chicken braised in a gravy made of yogurt, chicken broth, onion and butter

حمام محشى أرز/فريك
(hæ**mǣm** **mæ**ḥshi roz/ fi**rik**)
pigeon stuffed with cracked wheat or seasoned rice

برام حمـام
(bir**ǣm** ḥæ**mǣm**)
pigeon baked in a casserole with rice and milk (Egypt)

Vegetables

What vegetables do you recommend?	بأىّ الخضروات تنصح ؟	bi'æyy ælkhodrawāt tænsaḥ
أرز	roz	rice
باذنجان	bitingææn	aubergine (eggplant)
باميـة	bæmyæ	okra
باذلاء [بسلـة]	bisillæ	peas
بصـل	basal	onions
بطاطس	batātis	potatoes
ثـوم	tōm	garlic
جرجير	gærgīr	watercress
جزر	gazar	carrots
حمص	hommos	chick-peas
خرشوف [أرضى شوكى]	kharshūf [ardi shōki]	artichoke
خس	khass	lettuce
خيـار	khiyār	cucumber
ذرة	dora	Indian corn
سبانخ	sæbæænikh	spinach
طرشى [كبيس]	torshi [kæbīs]	gherkins
طماطم [بندورة]	tamātim [banadūra]	tomatoes
عـدس	'æds	lentils
فاصوليـا	fasolya	beans
لوبيا/خضراء/فول	lobyæ/khadra/fūl	string/green/black
فريـك	firīk [borgol]	cracked wheat
فجـل	figl	radishes
فلفـل أخضر	filfil akhdar	green peppers
قنبيط (أرنبيط)	arnabit	cauliflower
كرفس	karafs	celery
كرنب [ملفوف]	koromb [mælfūf]	cabbage
ورق عنب	wæræ' 'inæb	grape leaves

Vegetables may be served:

baked	فى الفرن	fil forn
boiled	مسلوق	mæslū'
chopped	مخرط	mikharrat
creamed	بالصلصة البيضاء	bil salsa ælbēda
diced	مكعبات	mokæ'æ bæt
fried	مقلى	mæ'li
grilled	مشوى	mæshwi
roasted	رستو	rosto
stewed	مسلوق	mosæbbæk
stuffed	محشى	mæḥshi

Vegetable dishes

ملوخية (molokhiyyæ) A very popular Egyptian dish is a spicy soup of greens flavoured with garlic. It's usually made with rice and chicken or meat.

مسقعة (mosækkæ'æ) Fried aubergine (eggplant) cooked with meat and raisins

محشى (mæḥshi) There's a variety of vegetables which fall into the category of *mahshees*. These are stuffed with a mixture of chopped meat (usually lamb or mutton), rice, onion and herbs. The most popular *mahshees* are the ones with grape leaves, green peppers, cabbage leaves, marrows (US zucchini), tomatoes and aubergine (eggplant). They can be eaten hot or cold and are usually served with yogurt.

لوبيا بزيت (lūbyæ bzēt) Green beans fried in oil, then braised in tomato sauce and served chilled with lemon (Lebanon)

بامية بالموزة (bæmyæ bil mōzæ) Okra braised in tomato sauce with beef knuckle

Fool

Fool is doubtless the favourite food preparation in the Middle East; its widespread popularity and its price put it on par with a hot-dog. *Fool* consists of black beans which have been cooked the previous night, seasoned with oil and lemon juice or served with butter. It may be served on a plate or in a bun. If you're in a hurry, stop at any *fool* restaurant and buy a *fool* or *falafel* sandwich.

فلافل (fælǣfil)	small balls of ground fool, mixed with greens and spices, fried in oil
بسارة (bisāra)	a purée made of ground fool, cooked with butter, and served with fried onions

Fool may also be eaten with Arab bread. Made of wheat- and Indian corn-flour, this tasty, flat, round bread replaces eating with utensils as it's used to scoop up food right from the bowl or plate.

Seeds, nuts, dried fruit

A major pastime in the Middle East seems to be cracking seeds. They're sold everywhere—near stadiums, at the cinema, on the streets and in the markets. The most common seed is from a variety of melon. Vendors of dried seeds also offer a choice of nuts and dried fruit.

dried seeds	محمصات	moḥammasāt
chestnuts	أبو فروة [كاستنة]	'æbū farwa [kæstænæ]
pecans	بكان	pikkǣn
hazelnuts	بندق	bondo'
nuts	جوز	gōz
walnuts	عين جمل	'ēn gæmæl
pistachio	فستق	fosto'
peanuts	فول سوداني	fūl sūdǣni
almonds	لوز	lōz

Fruit

The mild climate permits the cultivation of most of the fruit known in Europe as well as those from the tropics.

Do you have fresh fruit?	هل عندكم فواكه طازة؟	hæl ændokom fæwǣkih tāza
أنانـاس	'ænænǣs	pineapple
برتقال [ليمون]	borto'ǣn [læymūn]	orange
برقوق [خوخ]	bær'ū' [khōkh]	plums
بطيخ	battīkḥ	watermelon
بلح	bælæh	dates
تفـاح	tiffǣḥ	apples
تين	tīn	figs
جريب فروت	grēb frūt	grapefruit
جوافـة	gæwǣfæ	guava
جوز هندى	gōz hind	coconut
خوخ [دراء]	khōkh [darrā']	peach
رمـان	rommān	pomegranates
زبيب	zibīb	raisins
شمـام	shæmmǣm	melon
عنب (بنـاتى)	'inæb (bænǣti)	(seedless) grapes
فراولة	frawla	strawberries
قشطـة خضراء	'ishta khadra	custard apple, papaw
كـريز	krēz	cherries
كمثرى [نجاص]	kommitræ [nzhās]	pear
ليمون [حامض]	læmūn [ḥāmid]	lime
ليمون حلو	læmūn ḥilw	sweet lemon
مـانجة	mængæ	mangoes
مشمش	mishmish	apricots
مـوز	mōz	banana
يوسفندى [أفندى]	yosæfændī ['æfændī]	tangerines

EATING OUT

Dessert

If you've survived all the courses on the menu, you may want to say:

I'd like a dessert, please.	أريد حلوا من فضلك .	orīd ḥilw min fadlak
Something light, please.	شيء خفيف من فضلك .	shē' khæfīf min fadlak
Just a small portion.	مقدار صغير .	mikdār sagīr
Nothing more, thanks.	لا شيء آخر ، شكراً .	læ shē' 'ākhar shokran

If you aren't sure what to order, ask the waiter:

What do you have for dessert?	أى حلويات عندكم ؟	'æyy hælæwiyyæt ændokom
What do you recommend?	بم تنصح ؟	bimæ tansaḥ
cake	كيك	kēk
caramel custard	كريم كراميل	krēm karamil
fruit salad	فروت سالاد	frūt salad
ice-cream	أيس كريم	'æys krīm
rice pudding	أرز بلبن	roz bilæbæn
water-ice (sherbet)	جرانيطة [بوظة]	grānīta [būza]

Arabs have a sweet tooth for gooey, syrupy desserts like the well-known *baklava*. Some desserts even bear such fascinating names as Lady's Navel and Ali's Mother. These desserts are usually served with cream. If not, you can ask for your dessert:

with cream	بقشطة	bi'ishta

Here are some favourite Arabic desserts:

بسيمة (bæsīmæ)	semolina pudding baked with coconut and sugar

بقـلاوة (bæk**lǣ**wæ)	thin layers of pastry, filled with nuts, almonds and pistachios, steeped in syrup
بلح الشـام (bælæḥ ishsh**ǣm**)	"Syria's dates": puff pastry, fried, steeped in syrup
خشاف (khosh**ǣf**)	stewed fruit
صرة الست (so**rr**it issit)	"lady's navel": a ring-shaped sweet, steeped in syrup
عيش السراى ('ēsh æl sar**ā**yæ)	"palace bread": deep-fried sweet roll, steeped in syrup
قـرع عسلى (kar' 'æsæli)	pumpkin pudding with nuts, covered with a vanilla sauce; may be served hot or chilled
قطـايف (kat**ā**yif)	a pastry filled with nuts, fried and then topped with syrup
كـل واشكر (kol **woshkor**)	"eat it and thank God": smaller version of *baklava,* with less crust and more nuts, steeped in syrup
كنـافة (kon**ǣ**fæ)	pastry of thin fibres, baked with nuts or cream, steeped in syrup
أم على (om **ali**)	"Ali's mother", named after an Egyptian Mameluke queen; raisin cake, steeped in milk
بسبـوسة (bæsb**ū**sæ)	semolina tart, baked with butter, covered with syrup
مهلبيـة (mæhællæ**biyy**æ)	rice or Indian corn-flour pudding
ملبن [لكـوم] (**mæl**bæn [lo**kūm**])	Turkish delight

After a dinner including dessert and fruit, Arabs like to drink a cup of Turkish coffee. You'll certainly want to sample this world-renowned brew which will probably be the only type of coffee you'll be able to find. Turkish coffee is

EATING OUT

quite strong. It's boiled up three or more times in small, long-handled pots. When the coffee is served—grounds and all—let it sit a minute so that the grounds can settle to the bottom of the cup, and then sip only half the cup. You'll have to let the waiter know in advance whether or not you want your coffee sweetened, as the sugar and coffee are brewed together. Milk, sugar or cream aren't served with the coffee. Ask for:

Turkish coffee	قهوة تركى	'æhwæ torki

And according to how much sugar you want, say:

very sweet	سكر زيادة	sokkar ziyǣdæ
medium	مضبوط	mazbūt
without sugar	سادة	sǣdæ

That's the end of our Arabic menu. For wine and other drinks, see the following pages. But after the feast comes…

The bill (check)

May I have the bill (check), please?	أريد الحساب من فضلك .	orīd æl ḥisǣb min fadlak
Haven't you made a mistake?	ألا توجد غلطة ؟	'ælǣ tūgæd galta
Is service included?	هل هذا يشمل الخدمة ؟	hæl hǣzæ yæshmæl æl khidmæ
Is everything included?	هل هذا يشمل كل شيء ؟	hæl hǣzæ yæshmæl koll shē'
Do you accept traveller's cheques?	هل تقبل الشيكات السياحية ؟	hæl takbæl æl shēkǣt æl siyǣḥiyyæ
Thank you, this is for you.	شكراً ، هذا لك .	shokran hǣzæ læk
Keep the change.	احتفظ بالباقى .	'iḥtafiz bil bāki

That was a very good meal. We enjoyed it. Thank you.	كان الأكل عظيماً وأعجبنا جداً . شكراً .	**kǣ**næl 'ækl azīm wæ ææ**gæ**bænǣ **gid**dæn **sho**kran
We'll come again sometime.	سنأتي مرة ثانية ان شاء الله .	sænæ'tī marra tænyæ 'in shǣ'allāh

الخدمة محسوبة

SERVICE INCLUDED

Complaints

But perhaps you'll have something to complain about…

That's not what I ordered. I asked for…	هذا ليس ما طلبته . أنا طلبت ...	**hǣ**zæ **læ**ysæ mǣ ta**lab**to. 'ænǣ ta**labt**
I don't like this/ I can't eat this.	هذا لا يعجبني / لا يمكن أن آكل هذا .	**hǣ**zæ lǣ yo'giboni/læ **yom**kin 'æn '**ǣ**kol **hǣ**zæ
May I change this?	هل يمكن تغيير هذا ؟	hæl **yom**kin tæ**ġ**yīr **hǣ**zæ
The meat is…	اللحم ...	æl **læ**ḥm
overdone	شديد السواء	shæ**dīd** æl si**wæ**
underdone	قليل السواء	ka**līl** æl si**wæ**
too tough	ناشف جـداً	**nǣ**shif **gid**dæn
This is too…	هذا ... جداً .	**hǣ**zæ… **gid**dæn
bitter/salty/sweet	مرّ / مالح / مسكر	morr/**mǣ**liḥ/mi**sak**kar
The food is cold.	الأكل بارد .	æl 'ækl **bǣ**rid
This isn't fresh.	هذا ليس طازة .	**hǣ**zæ **læ**ysæ **tā**za
Would you ask the head waiter to come over?	اطلب من المتر الحضور من فضلك .	**ot**lob minæl **mitr** æl ḥo**dūr** min **fad**lak

EATING OUT

Drinks

Beer

Beer has been drunk in the Middle East as far back as the ancient Egyptians and Mesopotamians. Good beer is still brewed in the Middle East, and today in Egypt you can ask for Stella beer (**bi**ræ **still**æ), a light, lager beer, or an Aswan beer (**bi**rit as**wān**), a dark beer; Almaza (al**ma**za) and Laziza (la**zi**za) are noted brands in Lebanon.

Wine

The Middle East was doubtless the birthplace of wine. From biblical times to the eighth century A.D., vineyards flourished. But Islam forbids the drinking of wine, and production was sharply curtailed. In the last century, however, wine production was stepped up considerably.

The wine cellars of Ksara in Lebanon, founded by the Jesuits in 1857, are the largest in the Middle East. Egypt's Gianaclis vineyards on the Nile Delta at Abu Hummus are noted. Most of the wine is white but among the red is the remarkable Omar Khayyam which is full-bodied and has a curious aftertaste of dates.

You'll only be able to order wine in large restaurants, especially those specializing in foreign dishes catering to foreign clientele.

Omar Khayyam (red)	عمر خيام	**o**mar khæy**yǣm**
Ptolemy (white)	نبيذ البطالسة	ni**bīt** æl ba**ta**lsæ
Matameer (red)	نبيذ المطامير	ni**bīt** æl mata**mīr**
Gianaclis (red or white)	نبيذ جناكليس	ni**bīt** zhænæk**līs**
Queen Cleopatra (white)	نبيذ كليوباترة	ni**bīt** kilyo**ba**tra
Pharaoh's Wine (red)	نبيذ الفراعنة	ni**bit** æl fa**ra**'na

I'd like ... of wine.	أريد ... نبيذ .	orid ... nibīt
a bottle	زجـاجة	zogǣgit
half a bottle	نصف زجاجة	nisf zogǣgit
a glass	كبـاية	kobbæyit
I'd like something...	أريد شيئاً ...	orīd shæy'æn
sweet/sparkling/dry	حلواً/ بغازات/ جافا	ḥilw/bigæzǣt/gæf
I want a bottle of white wine.	أريد زجاجة نبيذ أبيض.	orīd zogǣgit nibīt 'abyad

red	أحمر	'aḥmar
white	أبيض	'abyad
rosé	روزيه	rozē

I don't want anything too sweet.	لا أريد شيئاً حلواً جداً .	lǣ orīd shē' ḥilw giddæn
How much is a bottle of...?	بكم زجاجة ... ؟	bikæm zogǣgit
Haven't you anything cheaper?	هل عندك شيء أرخص ؟	hæl 'ændæk shē' arkhas
Fine, that'll do.	هذا حسن .	hǣzæ ḥæsæn

If you enjoyed the wine, you may want to say:

Bring me another... please.	أريد ... آخر من فضلك .	orīd ... 'ākhar min fadlak
glass/bottle	كوب / زجاجة	kūb/zogǣgæ
What's the name of this wine?	ما اسم هذا النبيذ ؟	mæ 'ism hǣzæ æl nibīt
Where does this wine come from?	من أين ياتى هذا النبيذ ؟	min 'æynæ yæ'ti hǣzæ æl nibīt
How old is this wine?	ما عمر هذا النبيذ ؟	mæ 'omr hǣzæ æl nibīt

Other beverages

If you want some bottled mineral water, ask for *Sehha,* a mineral water from Lebanon.

I'd like some mineral water/a bottle of *Sehha.*	أريد ميـاه معدنية / زجاجة صحة .	orīd miyǣh mæ'dæniyyæ/ zogǣgit siḥḥa

With the great abundance of fruit available, fruit juice is a very popular drink in the Arab countries. Don't miss the opportunity to stop at one of the stands selling fruit juice which will be freshly squeezed for you. Lemon, sugar-cane and mango juice are the favourites.

I'd like a/an ... juice.	أريد عصير ...	orīd asir
apricot	مشمش	mishmish
carrot	جــزر	gazar
grape	عنب	'inæb
guava	جوافـة	gæwǣfæ
lemon	ليمون [حامض]	læmūn [ḥāmid]
mango	مـانجو	mængæ
orange	برتقـال	borto'ǣn
pomegranate	رمـان	rommān
strawberry	فراولـة	frawla
sugar-cane	قصب سكر	'asab sokkar
tamarind	تمر هنــدى	tamr hindi

A popular figure in Egypt is the *erkesoos* vendor, who walks the streets dressed in a colourful costume, calling attention to his presence by playing a type of finger bell. He'll gladly sell you a glass of *erkesoos* (a soft drink made from licorice) from the large bottle he carries. Just stop him and say:

I'd like a glass of *erkesoos,* please.	أريد كبـاية عرقسوس من فضلك .	orīd kobbǣyit 'irkisūs min fadlak

Coffee house

Going to a café in an Arab country is more than just for refreshment. It's a tradition. Inside or on the terrace, observing the drama of Arab street life, the atmosphere of the café is one of calm and cordiality.

While you can also order tea, soft drinks or mineral water, you'll undoubtedly want to try Turkish coffee. You've a choice: you can order it without sugar, sweet or very sweet.

Two other important activities in a café are smoking a water pipe or nargile and playing backgammon and dominoes. If you decide to try the water pipe, clap your hands to attract the waiter's attention, and ask him for a *nargile*. You'll have to tell him whether you want *tamback,* a natural coarse-cut tobacco, or *ma assil,* a lighter tobacco mixed with molasses.

The waiter will prepare the pipe and the tobacco, take the first puff to see that it's well lit, and then turn it over to you.

It's likely that a shoe-shine boy will offer to shine your shoes if you're a man but he won't do it for women!

When you're ready to leave, clap your hands and ask the waiter for the bill. For tipping, see inside back-cover.

I'd like a cup of...	أريد فنجان . . .	orīd fingǣn
coffee	قهوة	'æhwæ
tea	شاى	shǣy
mint tea	شاى بنعناع	shǣy bini'nǣæ
I'd like a water pipe.	أريد شيشة [أرجيلة] .	orīd shīshæ ['argīlæ]
Bring us a backgammon board/some dominoes, please.	نريد طاولة / دومينو من فضلك .	norīd tawla/domino min fadlak

FOR COFFEE, see also page 58

Eating light—Snacks

Stopping for a snack is a very popular thing to do in Arab countries, especially since their equivalent to our snackbars are open nearly all night. So, after the cinema, a football game or a concert, you can stop at a snack-bar to sample *fool, falafel* or *shawerma.*

Give me two of these and one of those.	اعطيني ٢ من هذه و ١ من هذه .	'aatini 'it**nēn** min hæ**zi**hi wæ **wǣ**ḥid min hǣ**zi**hi
to the left/to the right	الى الشمال / الى اليمين	'ilæ æshshi**mǣl**/'ilæl yæ**mīn**
above/below	الى أعلى / الى أسفل	'ilæ 'ææ**læ**/'ilæ 'æsfæl
I'd like a/an/some..., please.	أريد ... من فضلك .	o**rīd**... min **fad**lak
cheese sandwich	سندوتش جبنة	sændæ**witsh gib**næ
liver sandwich	سندوتش كبدة	sændæ**witsh kib**dæ
sausage sandwich	سندوتش سجق [معانق]	sændæ**witsh so**go' [mæ'**ǣ**nik]
roast beef sandwich	سندوتش روسبيف	sændæ**witsh** roz**bīf**
tongue sandwich	سندوتش لسان	sændæ**witsh** li**sǣn**
chicken sandwich	سندوتش فراخ	sændæ**witsh** fi**rǣkh**
baked macaroni, served with white sauce	مكرونة بالفرن	maka**rō**na bil forn
bread	خبز	khobz
butter	زبدة	**zib**dæ
cake	كيك	kēk
hamburger	همبرجر	ham**bor**gar
ice-cream	أيس كريم	'ǣys krīm
pastry	حلويات	ḥælæwiy**yǣt**
salad	صلاطة	sa**la**ta
How much is that?	بكم هذا ؟	bikæm **hǣ**zæ

Travelling around

The principal cities of Egypt—Cairo, Alexandria, Luxor and Aswan—are linked by regular flights. Because of their small area, Lebanon and Jordan aren't served by any domestic flights. At any airport you're sure to find someone who speaks English.

Do you speak English?	هل تتكلم الانجليزية ؟	hæl tætæ**kæ**llam ingi**lī**zi
Is there a flight to Amman?	هل توجد رحلة الى عمان ؟	hæl **tū**gæd **riḥ**læ ilæ 'æmmǣn
When's the next plane to Cairo?	ما موعد الطائرة القادمة الى القاهرة ؟	mǣ **mæw**'id æl tā'ira æl **kā**dimæ ilǣ ælkāhira
Can I make a connection to Beirut?	هل أستطيع أن أعمل امتداد الى بيروت ؟	hæl asta**tī** æn æ'mil 'imti**dǣd** ilǣ **bæy**rūt
I'd like a ticket to Damascus.	أريد تذكرة لدمشق .	o**rīd** tæzkara li di**mishk**
What's the fare to Luxor?	ما الثمن الى الأقصر ؟	mǣ æl **tæ**mæn ilǣ **lok**sor
single (one-way)	ذهاب	zi**hǣb**
return (roundtrip)	ذهاب و اياب	zi**hǣb** wæ 'i**yǣb**
What time does the plane take off?	متى تقوم الطائرة ؟	mæ**tǣ** tæ**kūm** æl tā'ira
What time do I have to check in?	متى يجب أن أقدم نفسى فى المطار ؟	mæ**tǣ** **yæ**gib æn o**kad**dim **næf**si fil ma**tār**
What's the flight number?	ما نمرة الرحلة ؟	mǣ **nim**rit æl **riḥ**læ
What time do we arrive?	متى نصل ؟	mæ**tǣ** na**sill**

وصول ARRIVAL	رحيل DEPARTURE

Bus

Buses and taxis are the most important means of transportation in the Middle East. City buses provide a regular, if crowded, service. Cities are linked by ordinary and express services. Express buses are comfortable and very reasonably priced.

It isn't advisable to travel by bus in the big cities during the rush hours: buses are so overcrowded that you would have to hang on to the outside! If you are in Lebanon it might be better to try a collective taxi (called a *service*—særvis—in Arabic). A *service* will wait until it's full, and will then follow the regular bus route. These collective taxis operate in all major cities. Only slightly more expensive than the bus, they are often more convenient.

In Egypt collective taxis ply between Cairo and Alexandria. They leave from the railway station.

City buses show their destinations in Arabic and their route numbers in our figures. When you plan to take a bus the best thing is to ask your hotel desk clerk for directions.

City buses don't follow any set schedule. Buses run frequently, so just go to the bus stop and wait. Your bus is bound to come along soon. Interurban buses, on the other hand, do have time-tables.

Inquiries

I'd like a bus pass.	أريد اشتراك أوتوبيس .	orīd ishtirāk otobis
Where can I get a bus/a collective taxi to...?	أين أجد أوتوبيس / تاكسى مشترك الى ... ؟	aynæ 'ægid otobīs/tæksi moshtarak 'ilæ
What bus do I take to Abou-Kir?	أى أوتوبيس أركب الى أبى قير ؟	æyy otobīs ærkæb ilæ 'æbūkīr

FOR TAXI, see page 27

What number is it to...?	ما النمرة للذهاب الى ...؟	mǣ æl **nim**ræ lil **zi**hǣb ilǣ
Where's the...?	أين ... ؟	æynæ
bus station	موقف الأوتوبيس	**maw**kif æl 'oto**bīs**
bus stop	محطة الأوتوبيس	ma**ḥat**tit æl 'oto**bīs**
When's the ... bus to Amman?	متى يقوم الأوتوبيس ... الى عمان ؟	mætǣ ya**kūm** æl 'oto**bīs**... ilǣ '**æm**mǣn
first/last/next	الأول / الأخير / القادم	æl '**æw**wæl/æl 'æ**khīr**/æl **kā**dim
Do I have to change buses?	هل يجب أن أغير الأوتوبيس ؟	hæl **yæ**gib æn o**gæy**yir æl 'oto**bīs**
How long does the journey take?	ما مدة الرحلة ؟	mæ **mod**dit æl **riḥ**læ

Tickets

Where's the information office?	أين مكتب الاستعلامات ؟	**æy**næ **mæk**tæb æl '**is**ti'læmǣt
Where can I buy a ticket?	أين أشترى التذكرة ؟	**æy**næ æsh**tæ**ri æl taz**ka**ra
I want a ticket to Cairo.	أريد تذكرة للقاهرة .	o**rīd** taz**ka**ra lil kā**hi**ra
I'd like 2 singles to El Mansura.*	أريد تذكرتين ذهاب للمنصورة .	o**rīd** tazkar**tēn** zi**hæb** lil man**sū**ra
How much is the fare to Alexandria?	بكم التذكرة للاسكندرية ؟	bi**kæm** æl **taz**kara lil 'æskændæ**riy**yæ
Is it half price for a child? He's/She's 13.	هل أدفع نصف تذكرة للطفل ؟ سنه/سنها ١٣سنة.	hæl **æd**fæ' nisf taz**ka**ra lil tifl? **sin**no/sin**næ**hæ 13 **sæ**næ

Note: Children up to the age of five travel free.

* see grammar

FOR NUMBERS, see page 175

ذهاب أم ذهاب واياب ؟	Single or return (one-way or roundtrip)?
تدفع نصف تذكرة حتى سن . . .	It's half price up to the age of...
يجب أن تدفع تذكرة كاملة.	You'll have to pay full fare.

All aboard

Excuse me. May I get by?	آسف . أريد المرور .	ǣsif. o**rīd** æl mo**rūr**
Is this seat taken?	هل هذا الكرسى محجوز ؟	hæl **hǣ**zæl **kor**si **mæḥ**gūz
Is this seat free?	هل هذا الكرسى فاضى ؟	hæl **hǣ**zæl **kor**sī **fā**di

ممنوع التدخين
NO SMOKING

I think that's my seat.	أظن أن هذا الكرسى لى .	a**zonn** æn**næ** **hǣ**zæl **kor**si lī
Can you tell me when we get to Memphis?	متى نصل الى ممفيس من فضلك ؟	mæ**tǣ** **na**sil i**lǣ** **mæm**fis min **fad**lak
What station is this?	ما هذه المحطة ؟	mǣ hǣ**zi**hi æl ma**ḥat**ta
Will you tell me when to get off?	قل لى متى أنزل من فضلك .	ʼolli mæ**tǣ** æn**zil** min **fad**lak
I want to get off at Khan El-Khalili.	أريد النزول عند خان الخليلى .	o**rīd** æl no**zūl** **in**da khǣn æl**khæ**līlī
Please let me off at the next stop.	من فضلك أنزلنى فى المحطة الجاية .	min **fad**lak æn**zil**ni fil ma**ḥat**ta æl **gǣ**yyæ
May I have my luggage, please?	أريد شنطتى من فضلك .	o**rīd** shan**ti**ti min **fad**lak

Train

What few passenger trains run in Jordan and Lebanon are slow and uncomfortable. Egypt, on the other hand, has a modern railway system with express trains. Fares are cheap, and trains are comfortable. During high season, it's advisable to reserve seats ahead of time.

Trains in Egypt generally have a dining-car, while sometimes hot meals can be served right at your seat. The steward will pass through the car to take your order. Usually, there's a set menu. You can also order drinks and sandwiches from him.

If you're in a hurry, take an air conditioned express train (with first and second class) which links major cities. For long trips, you can reserve a berth or compartment in a sleeping-car.

Children travel free up to the age of five and pay half-fare from six to ten. Note that at the railway station, ticket windows are segregated according to sex—and that the queue for women is generally shorter...

درجة أولى	FIRST CLASS
درجة ثانية	SECOND CLASS

To the station

Where's the railway station?	أين محطة السكة الحديد ؟	æynæ ma**ḥ**attit æl **sik**kæ æl **ḥ**ædid
Taxi, please!	تاكسى !	**tæ**ksi
Take me to the railway station.	خذنى الى محطة السكة الحديد .	**khod**ni ilæ ma**ḥ**attit æl **sik**kæ æl **ḥ**ædid

Inquiries

How much is the fare to Suez?	بكم التذكرة الى السويس ؟	bikæm æl tazkara ilǣ ælsiwês
Is it a through train?	هل هو قطار مباشر ؟	hæl howæ kitār mobǣshir
Does the train stop at Al Minya?	هل يتوقف القطار في المنيا ؟	hæl yætæwakkaf æl kitār fil minyæ
When is the ... train to Aswan?	متى يقوم القطار ... الى أسوان ؟	mætǣ yækūm æl kitār... ilǣ aswān
first/last/next	الأول / الأخير / القادم	æl 'æwwæl/æl 'ækhīr/æl kādim
What time does the train from Damascus arrive?	متى يصل القطار القادم من دمشق ؟	mætǣ yasil æl kitār æl kādim min dimishk
What time does the train for Alexandria leave?	متى يقوم قطار الاسكندرية؟	mætǣ yakūm kitār æl 'æskændæriyyæ
Is the train late?	هل القطار متأخر ؟	hæl æl kitār motæ'ækhkhir
Is there a dining-car/ sleeping-car on the train?	هل توجد في القطار عربة طعام / عربة نوم ؟	hæl tūgæd fil kitār 'arabit ta'ām/'arabit nōm

دخول	ENTRANCE
خروج	EXIT
الى الرصيف	TO THE PLATFORMS

Platform (track)

What platform does the train for Suez leave from?	من أى رصيف يقوم قطار السويس ؟	min æyy rasīf yakūm kitār ælsiwês
Where is platform 4?	أين رصيف ٤ ؟	æynæ rasīf 4
Is this the right platform for the train to Port-Saïd?	هل هذا هو الرصيف المضبوط لقطار بور سعيد ؟	hæl hǣzæ howæ æl rasīf æl mazbūt likitār bōr sa'īd

FOR TAXI, see page 27

انه قطار مباشر .	It's a direct train.
يجب أن تغير فى ...	You have to change at...
درجة أولى أم ثانية ؟	First or second class?
رصيف ... موجود ...	Platform ... is ...
هناك / تحت	over there/downstairs
على الشمال / على اليمين	on the left/on the right
قطار ... يقوم الساعة ... على رصيف ...	The train to ... will leave at ... from platform ...

Where's the ... ?

Where's the...?	أين ... ؟	æynæ
left luggage office	مكتب الأمانات	**mæk**tæb æl 'æmæ**næt**
lost property (lost and found) office	مكتب المفقودات	**mæk**tæb æl **mæf**kūdæt
newsstand	كشك الجرائد	koshk æl gar**ā**'id
restaurant	مطعم	**mat**'am
ticket office	شباك التذاكر	shib**bæk** æl tæz**æ**kir
waiting room	صالة الانتظار	**sā**lit æl **in**tizār

Boat

Boats and steamers ply up and down the Nile. A trip on one of these magnificent, luxury steamers is well worthwhile. These boats are very chic and comfortable. You can take a relaxing one- or two-week cruise on one of them. From Cairo to Luxor takes about two weeks while the voyage from Aswan to Luxor or vice-versa lasts about a week.

The steamers put in at several ports, affording the opportunity to make land excursions. Tickets sold through travel

FOR TICKETS, see page 67

agents include full board on the ship plus an air ticket from Cairo to Aswan or Luxor. Local travel agents will advise you about sailing dates, which are usually once weekly or every two weeks.

There's also a one-day excursion by hydrofoil from Aswan to the ancient temple of Abu-Simbel with its enormous statue of Ramses II. Enquire about it at your hotel or travel agent's. In Cairo you can take a water-bus which you'll find quite pleasant.

When's the next steamer sailing for Luxor?	متى تقوم الباخرة القادمة الى الأقصر ؟	**mæ**tǣtæ**kūm**ælbǣ**khi**raæl **kā**dimæ **ilǣ** **lok**sor
I'd like to book passage for 2 to Aswan.*	أريد أن أحجز تذكرتين لأسوان .	o**rīd** æn **æḥ**giz tæzkar**tēn** li'**as**wān
I want a return (roundtrip) ticket on the hydrofoil to the Abu-Simbel temple.	أريد تذكرة ذهاب وإياب الى معبد أبو سمبل على الهيدروفيل .	o**rīd** tazkara zi**hǣb** wæ 'i**yāb** ilǣ **mæ**æbæd abū**sim**bil ælæl hidrō**fīl**

Other means of transportation

bicycle	عجلة [بسيكليت]	ægælæ [bisi**klēt**]
camelback riding	ركوب الجمل	ro**kūb** æl **gæ**mæl
helicopter	هليكوبتر	hili**kob**tar
hitchhiking	أوتوستوب	oto**stop**
horseback riding	ركوب الخيل	ro**kūb** æl **khēl**
moped (motorbike)	دراجة بخارية	dar**rā**gæ bokhǣ**riy**yæ
motorcycle	موتوسيكل	moto**sikl**

And if you're really stuck, start...

walking	امشى	**'im**shi

* see grammar

TRAVELLING AROUND

Around and about—Sightseeing

Here we're more concerned with the cultural aspect of life than with entertainment; and, for the moment, with towns rather than the countryside.

Can you recommend a good guide book on...?	من فضلك انصحنى بدليل سياحى جيد عن ...	min **fad**lak in**saḥ**nī bidæ**līl** si**yǣ**ḥī gæy**yid** 'æn
Where's the tourist office?	أين مكتب السياحة ؟	æynæ **mæk**tæb æl si**yǣ**ḥæ
What are the main points of interest?	ما أهم المعالم السياحية ؟	mǣ 'æ**hæm** æl mæ'**ǣ**lim æl siyæ**ḥīy**yæ
We're here for...	سنبقى هنا ...	sæ**nab**kā **honǣ**
only a few hours	بضعة ساعات فقط	**bid**'at sǣ'**ǣt** **fa**kat
a day	يـوم	yōm
3 days	٣ أيـام	3 æy**yǣm**
a week	أسبوع	**os**bū
Can you recommend a (city) sightseeing tour?	من فضلك انصحنى بجولة سياحية (للمدينة) .	min **fad**lak in**saḥ**nī bi**gæw**læ si**yǣ**ḥiyyæ (lilmæ**dī**næ)
Where does the bus start from?	من أين يبدأ الأوتوبيس ؟	min æynæ **yæb**dæ' æl 'oto**bīs**
Will it pick us up at the hotel?	هل سيأخذنا من الفندق ؟	hæl sæyæ'**khoz**nǣ min æl **fon**dok
What bus/tram (street-car) should we take?	ما الأوتوبيس / الترام الذى نركبه ؟	mǣ æl 'oto**bīs**/æl **tirām** æl**læ**zī nær**kabo**
How much does the tour cost?	ما ثمن الجولة ؟	mǣ **tæ**mæn æl **gæw**læ
What time does the tour start?	متى تبدأ الجولة ؟	mætǣ **tæb**dæ' æl **gæw**læ
We'd like to rent a car for the day.	نريد تأجير سيارة ليوم .	no**rīd** tæ'**gīr** say**yāra** li**yōm**
Is there an English-speaking guide?	هـل يوجد مرشد سياحى يتكلم الانجليزية ؟	hæl **yū**gæd **mor**shid si**yǣ**ḥi yætæ**kæl**læm æl 'ingi**lī**ziyyæ

FOR TIME OF DAY, see page 178

Where is/Where are the...?	أين ... ؟	æynæ
abbey	الـدير	æl dēr
amusement park	مدينة الملاهى	mædinæt æl mælæhi
aquarium	حديقة الأسماك	ḥædīkat æl 'æsmæk
art gallery	قاعـة الفنون	kā'æt æl fonūn
artists' quarter	حى الفنانين	ḥæyy æl fænnænīn
bazaar	السوق [البازار]	æl sūk [æl bazār]
beach	الشاطىء	æl shāti'
botanical gardens	الحديقة النباتية	æl ḥædīka æl næbættiyyæ
bridge	الكوبرى [الجسر]	æl kobrī [æl zhisr]
building	المبـنى	æl mæbnæ
business district	حى الأعمال	ḥæyy æl 'æemæl
basilica	البازيليك	æl bæzilīk
castle	القصر	æl kasr
catacombs	سراديب الأموات	særædīb æl mæwtæ
cathedral	الكاتدرائية	æl kætidrā'iyyæ
citadel	القلعـة	æl kalaa
city centre	وسط المدينة	wasat æl mædīnæ
city hall	مبنى المحافظة	mæbnæ æl moḥāfza
church	الكنيسة	æl kænīsæ
concert hall	قاعة الموسيقى	ka'æt æl mosīka
convent	الدير	æl dēr
docks	أرصفة الميناء	arsifat æl mīnæ
downtown area	وسط المدينة	wasat æl mædīnæ
exhibition	المعرض	æl maarad
factory	المصنع	æl masnaa
fortress	الحصن	æl ḥisn
fountain	النافورة	æl nafūra
gardens	الحدائق	æl hædæ'ik
harbour	الميـنـاء	æl mīnæ
lake	البحيرة	æl boḥæyra
library	المكتبة	æl mæktæbæ

FOR ASKING THE WAY, see page 143

market	السوق	æl sūk
monastery	الدير	æl dēr
monument	النصب التذكارى	æl nasb æl tizk**ǣ**ri
mosque	الجامع	æl **gǣ**mi'
museum	المتحف	æl **mæt**ḥ**ǣ**f
observatory	المرصد	æl **mar**sad
old city	المدينة القديمة	æl mæ**dī**næ æl ka**dī**mæ
opera house	دار الأوبرا	dār æl **o**birā
palace	القصر	æl kasr
park	الحديقة	æl ḥæ**dī**ka
parliament building	مبنى البرلمان	**mæb**næ æl barla**mān**
presidential palace	القصر الجمهورى	æl kasr æl gum**hū**ri
pyramids	الأهرام	æl **ah**rām
river	النهر	æl nahr
royal palace	القصر الملكى	æl kasr æl **mæ**læki
ruins	الأطلال	æl **at**lāl
seafront	شاطىء البحر	**shā**ti' æl baḥr
shopping centre	المركز التجارى	æl **mær**kæz æl to**gǣ**ri
sphinx	أبو الهول	**abul** hōl
stadium	الأستاد	æl **'is**tǣd
statue	التمثال	æl **tim**sǣl
stock exchange	البورصة	æl **bor**sa
swimming pool	حمام السباحة [البسين]	hæm**mǣm** æl si**bǣ**ḥæ [pisīn]
synagogue	المعبد اليهودى	æl **mæ**æbæd æl yæ**hū**dī
temple	المعبد	æl mææ**bæd**
theatre	المسرح	æl **mas**raḥ
tomb	القبر	æl kabr
tower	البرج	æl borg
university	الجامعة	æl **gæm**'æ
walls	سور المدينة	sūr æl mæ**dī**næ
zoo	حديقة الحيوان	ḥæ**dī**kat æl ḥæyæ**wǣn**

Admission

Is the ... open on Fridays/Sundays?	هــل الـ ... مفتوح يوم الجمعة / الأحد ؟	hæl æl...mæftūḥ yōm æl **gomaa**/æl 'æḥæd
When does it open?	متى يفتح ؟	mætā yæftæḥ
When does it close?	متى يغلق [يقفل] ؟	mætā yoglak
How much is the admission charge?	بكم الدخول ؟	bikæm æl dokhūl
Is there any reduction for students/children?	هل يوجد تخفيض للطلبة / للأطفال ؟	hæl yūgæd takhfīd liltalaba/lil'atfāl
Have you a guide book in English?	هل عندك دليــل سياحى بالانجليزية ؟	hæl indæk dælīl siyæḥi bil 'ingilīziyyæ
Can I buy a catalogue?	هل أستطيــع أن أشترى كتالوج ؟	hæl astatī' æn æshtæri kætælōg
Do you have any postcards?	هل عندك كروت ؟	hæl indæk korūt
Is it all right to take pictures?	هل أستطيع التصوير ؟	hæl æstatī' æl taswīr

الدخول مجانى	ADMISSION FREE
ممنوع التصوير	NO CAMERAS ALLOWED

Who—What—When?

What's that building?	ما هذا المبنى ؟	mæ hæzæ æl mæbnæ
Who was the...?	من كـان ...؟	mæn kæn
architect	المهندس	æl mohændis
artist	الفنــان	æl fænnæn
painter	الرسام	æl ræssæm
sculptor	النحات	æl næḥḥæt

Who built it?	من بناه؟	mæn bæ**nææh**
Who painted that picture?	من رسم هذه الصورة؟	mæn **ræsæm hææzihi** æl **süra**
When did he live?	متى عاش ؟	**mætææ ææsh**
When was it built?	متى تم البناء ؟	**mætææ tæmmæ** æl bi**nææ'**
Where's the house where ... lived?	أين المنزل الذى عاش فيه ... ؟	**æy**næ æl **mæn**zil æl**læ**zi **ææ**shæ fih
We're interested in...	نحن مهتمين بـ ...	**næḥ**no mohtæm**mīn** bi
antiques	الأنتيكات	æl æntikæt
archeology	الآثار	æl ā**sār**
art	الفن	æl fæn
botany	النباتات	æl næbææ**tææt**
ceramics	الفخار	æl fokh**khār**
coins	العملات	æl 'om**lææt**
crafts	العمل اليدوى	æl 'æmæl æl **yæ**dæwi
fine arts	الفنون الجميلة	æl fo**nūn** æl gæ**mī**læ
folk art	الفنون الشعبية	æl fo**nūn** æl shæ'**biy**yæ
furniture	الفرش [الموبيليا]	æl færsh [æl mo**bil**yæ]
geology	الجيولوجيا	æl zhiyo**lo**zhiæ
hieroglyphics	الهيروغليفيات	æl hiroglī**fiy**yææt
history	التاريخ	æl tææ**rīkh**
local crafts	الفنون المحلية	æl fo**nūn** æl mæḥæl**liy**yæ
medicine	الطب	æl tibb
music	الموسيقى	æl mūsīka
painting	الرسم	æl ræsm
pottery	الغزف	æl **khæ**zæf
prehistory	ما قبل التاريخ	mææ kabl æl tææ**rīkh**
sculpture	النحت	æl næḥt
zoology	علم الحيوان	ilm æl ḥæyæ**wææn**
Where's the ... department?	أين قسم ... ؟	**æy**næ kism

Just the adjective you've been looking for...

It's...	هذا ...	hææzæ
amazing	مدهش	modhish
awful	مخيف	mokhīf
beautiful	جميل	gæmīl
excellent	ممتاز	momtææz
interesting	مهم	mohim
magnificent	عظيم	azīm
monumental	عظيم	azīm
sinister	مشئوم	mæsh'ūm
strange	غريب	gærīb
stupendous	هائل	hææ'il
superb	بديع	bædī'
terrible	مخيف	mokhīf
terrifying	مفزع	mofzi'
tremendous	هائل	hææ'il

Religious services

Islam is the religion of 90 per cent of the population of the Middle East, although Lebanon is almost evenly divided between Moslems and Christians. Among the Christian denominations, the Coptic Church is the largest with over six million adherents. Eastern Orthodox and Uniate Catholic churches are also found throughout the area. Small Protestant and Jewish groups exist in many Arab cities.

The faith of nearly 700 million people, Islam is the youngest of the world's great religions. The Koran represents the written revelations of God to the prophet Mohammed, and many of its greatest precepts parallel those of the Bible. In fact, Islam acknowledges the validity of Christian and Jewish teachings.

Spread principally through North Africa, the Middle East and large parts of Asia, Islam is divided into two major bodies plus many sects. But among the basic practices which should be followed by all Moslems are prayer five times daily facing Mecca, fasting during the sacred month of Ramadan, almsgiving and at least one pilgrimage to Mecca during the lifetime of each Moslem. The Koran forbids eating pork, drinking alcohol and gambling, but just as in the Christian West, modern life is bringing about a more relaxed attitude towards the observance of these practices.

Mosques are always open to visitors, except during worship. Picture-taking is permitted. The floors of the mosques are covered with beautifully-woven prayer rugs. To avoid soiling them, visitors and worshippers alike must remove their shoes before entering. At large mosques, over-sized slippers are available to visitors. If you make use of them it's customary to give the attendant a small tip. Don't wear shorts, miniskirts or bare-shouldered blouses in the mosque, and remember not to walk in front of people who are in prayer.

Is there a/an... near here?	هل يوجد.. قريب من هنا؟	hæl **yū**gæd ... ka**rīb** min **ho**nǣ
Catholic church	كنيسة كاثوليكية	ki**nī**sæ kætōli**kiy**yæ
Orthodox church	كنيسة أورثودوكس	ki**nī**sæ ortodo**ksiy**yæ
Protestant church	كنيسة بروتستنت	ki**nī**sæ protis**tant**
mosque	جامع	gǣ**mi'**
synagogue	معبد يهودى	mææ**bæd** yæ**hū**di
At what time are the services?	ما هى مواقيت الصلاة ؟	mǣ **hi**yæ mæwā**kīt** æl sa**lāh**

Relaxing

Cinema (movies)—Theatre

There are many open-air cinemas operating from June to September which have double- or triple-feature programmes after sundown. The conventional indoor cinema has a feature film preceded by a newsreel, a documentary and commercials.

In both Egypt and Lebanon, American and English films are very popular and are shown in their original versions. In Egypt, the first showing normally starts at 3.30 p.m. except on Sundays and Fridays when there's a matinee at 10.30 a.m.

Theatre curtain time is usually 9.30 p.m. Booking in advance is a must. You can find out what's on by consulting the newspapers or publications of the type "This Week in..."

A renowned marionette show performs at special theatres in Egypt to the delight of young and old alike.

Have you the most recent "This Week in..."?	هل عندك آخر عدد من الأسبوع فى ... ؟	hæl **æn**dæk **ǣ**khir æ**d**æd min æl '**os**bū fī
What's on at the cinema tonight?	ما هى الأفلام مساء اليوم ؟	mǣ **hi**yæ æl 'æf**lǣm** mi**sǣ'** æl yōm
What's playing at the theatre?	ما هى المسرحيات ؟	mǣ **hi**yæ æl masraḥiy**yǣt**
What sort of play is it?	ما نوع المسرحية ؟	mǣ nō' æl masra**ḥiy**ya
Who's it by?	من المؤلف ؟	mæn æl mo'**æl**lif
Where's that new film by ... playing?	أين يدور فيلم... الجديد ؟	**æy**næ yæ**dūr** film...æl gæ**dīd**

Can you recommend (a) ...?	هل تنصحنى بـ . . . ؟	hæl tæn**saḥ**ni bi
good film	فيلم جيد	film gæy**yid**
comedy	كوميديا	komidyæ
drama	دراما	**drā**ma
musical	أوبريت	obē**rēt**
revue	عرض فنى	ard **fæ**nni
thriller	فيلم بوليسى	film bo**lī**si
Western	فيلم رعاة البقر	film ro**ǣt** æl **ba**kar
I'd like to see a puppet show.	أريد أن أشاهد عرضا للعرائس .	o**rīd** æn o**shǣ**hid ard lil **ara**'is
What time does it begin?	متى يبدأ ؟	**mæ**tǣ **yæb**dæ'
What time does the show end?	متى ينتهى العرض ؟	mætǣ yæn**tæ**hī æl 'ard
What time does the first evening performance start?	متى تبدأ أول حفلة فى المساء ؟	mætǣ **tæb**dæ' **æw**wæl **ḥæ**flæ fil mæ**sǣ**'
Are there any tickets for tonight?	هل توجد تذاكر لليلة ؟	hæl **tū**gæd tæ**zǣ**kir lil **lē**læ
I want to reserve 2 tickets for the show on Saturday evening.*	أريد أن أحجز تذكرتين لحفلة يوم السبت مساء .	o**rīd** æn **æḥ**giz tazkar**tēn** li**ḥæ**flit yōm æl sæbt mæ**sǣ**'æn
Can I have a ticket for the matinee on Tuesday?	أريد تذكرة للحفلة الماتينية يوم الثلاثاء .	o**rīd** taz**ka**ra lil **ḥæ**flæ æl mæti**nē** yōm æl solæ**sǣ**'
I want a seat in the stalls (orchestra).	أريد مكانا فى الصالة .	o**rīd** mæ**kǣn** fil **sā**la
Not too far back.	ليس الى الوراء كثيرا .	**læy**sæ i**lǣ** æl wa**rā**' kæ**sī**ran

* see grammar

Opera—Ballet—Concert

Don't miss the opportunity to attend Middle Eastern music and dancing performances. At Lebanon's Baalbek ruins ballets and concerts are held in the temple of Bacchus where local and internationally known artists perform. Among sound-and-light shows, you'll not want to miss the impressive production given at the Pyramids and the Citadel in Cairo and in Karnak.

In Beirut and Cairo you can also go to recitals and symphony concerts performed by both local and visiting artists.

Where's the opera house?	أين دار الأوبرا ؟	æynæ dār æl 'obira
Where's the concert hall?	أين صالة الموسيقى ؟	æynæ sālit æl mūsīka
What's on at the opera tonight?	ماذا فى الأوبرا مساء اليوم؟	mæzæ fi æl 'obira mæsæ' æl yōm
Who's singing?	من يغنى ؟	mæn yogænni
Who's dancing?	من يرقص ؟	mæn yærkos
What time does the programme start?	متى يبدأ البرنامج ؟	mætæ yæbdæ' æl birnæmig
What orchestra is playing?	ما الفرقة التى تعزف ؟	mæ æl firka æl læti tææz
What are they playing?	ماذا يعزفون ؟	mæzæ yææzifūn
Who's the conductor?	من رئيس الفرقة ؟	mæn ra'is æl firka

آسف لا توجد أية مقاعد .	I'm sorry, we're sold out.
لم يبق سوى بعض المقاعد فى البلكون .	There are only a few seats in the balcony (circle).
أريد أن أرى تذكرتك من فضلك .	May I see your ticket?

Night clubs

Night clubs are pretty much the same the world over, particularly when it comes to inflated prices. For most night clubs jacket and tie are sufficient.

In Beirut, the night clubs have a decidedly French flavour. If you only visit one night club during your visit, make sure the floor show features belly-dancers.

Can you recommend a good night club?	هل تنصحنى بملهى ليلى جيد ؟	hæl tan**saḥ**ni bi **mæl**hǣ **læ**yli **gæy**yid
Is there a floor show?	هل يوجد عرض فنى ؟	hæl **yū**gæd 'ard **fæn**ni
Are there belly-dancers?	هل توجد راقصات شرقية ؟	hæl **tū**gæd rāki**sāt** shar**kiy**ya
What time does the floor show start?	متى يبدأ العرض الفنى ؟	**mæ**tǣ **yæb**dæ' æl 'ard æl **fæn**ni
Is evening dress necessary?	هل لبس السهرة ضرورى ؟	hæl libs æl **sah**ra da**rū**ri

And once inside ...

A table for 2, please.	ترابيزة [طاولة] لـ ٢ من فضلك .	tara**bē**zæ [**taw**la] li 2 min **fad**lak
My name's... I booked a table for 4.	اسمى ... لقد حجزت ترابيزة [طاولة] لـ ٤ .	**is**mi...la**kad** ḥæ**gæzt** tara**bē**za [**taw**la] li 4
We haven't got a reservation.	ليس عندنا حجز .	**læy**sæ **in**dænǣ ḥægz

FOR NUMBERS, see page 175

Dancing

Where can we go dancing?	أين يمكن الذهاب للرقص ؟	æynæ yomkin æl zihææb lil raks
Is there a discotheque anywhere here?	هل توجد مراقص هنا ؟	hæl tūgæd marākis honā
There's a ball at the...	هناك حفلة فى ...	honāk ḥæflæ fi
Would you like to dance?	هل ترقصين ؟	hæl tærkosīn
May I have this dance?	هــل تسمحى لى بهذه الرقصة ؟	hæl tæsmaḥi li bihææzihi æl raksa

Do you happen to play ... ?

On rainy days, this page may solve your problems.

Do you happen to play chess?	هل تلعب الشطرنج ؟	hæl tæl'æb shatarang
I'm afraid I don't.	آسف لا ألعب .	āsif lǣ 'æl'æb
No, but I'll give you a game of back-gammon/domino.	لا . ولكنى أستطيع أن ألعب الطاولة / الدومينو	lǣ wæ lækinni astatī' æn 'ǣl'æb æl tawla/æl domino
king	ملك	mælik
queen	وزير	wæzīr
castle (rook)	طابية	tabya
bishop	فيــل	fil
knight	حصان [فرس]	ḥosān [faras]
pawn	عسكرى [بيدق]	æskæri [bēdæ']
Check mate!	كش مات !	kishsh mǣt
Do you play cards?	هل تلعب ورق [كوتشينة] ؟	hæl tæl'æb wæræk [kotshīnæ]
ace	آس	ǣs
king	شايب [روا]	shǣyib [rwā]
queen	بنت	bint
jack	ولد	wælæd
joker	جوكر	zhōkar

spades	بستوني	bæstōni
hearts	كوبا	kobba
diamonds	ديناري	dinæri
clubs	سباتي	sobæti

Though gambling is forbidden by the Koran, casinos are operated all-year round in the Middle East for free-spending foreigners. To enter a casino, you must be over 21 and show your passport. When in Lebanon, visit the *Casino du Liban,* claimed to rival the casino of Monte Carlo. Lebanon's casino palace is found 13 miles from Beirut at Maalmeltein.

Oriental chess

In the Middle East, a very popular game is oriental chess, or backgammon, called *tawla* in Arabic. Shown below is the backgammon board. The game is played with dice. The winner is he who first has all his counters on his side.

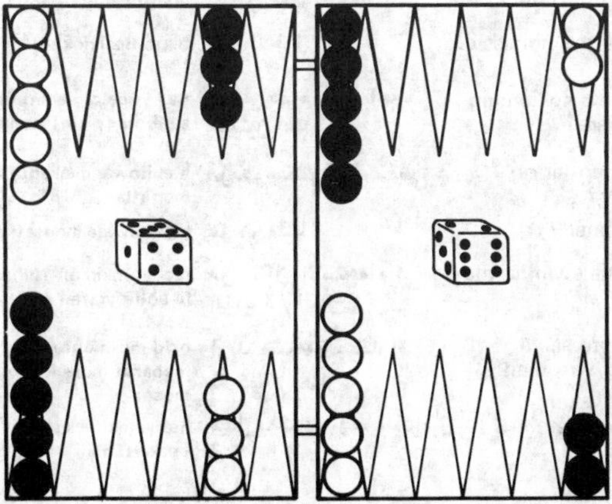

Sport

Football (soccer) is probably the favourite sport in the Middle East, especially in Egypt, but basketball, tennis and water sports are also very popular. Given the temperate-to-hot climate, water sports are practiced enthusiastically on the Mediterranean coastlines of Egypt and Lebanon and on the Nile. There is horse-racing on Saturdays and Sundays in Egypt.

Where's the nearest golf course?	أين أقرب ملعب جولف ؟	æynæ **ak**rab mæl'**æb** golf
Can we hire (rent) clubs?	هل يمكن تأجير العصيان ؟	hæl **yom**kin tæ'**gīr** æl 'os**yān**
Where are the tennis courts?	أين ملاعب التنس ؟	æynæ mæ**lǣ**'ib æl **ti**nis
Can I hire rackets?	هل يمكن تأجير المضارب ؟	hæl **yom**kin tæ'**gīr** æl madārib
What's the charge per...?	ما الثمن لمدة ... ؟	mǣ æl **tæ**mæn li**mod**dæt
day/round/hour	يوم / لفة / ساعة	yōm/**læf**fæ/**sǣ**'æ
What's the admission charge?	بكم الدخول ؟	bi**kæm** æl do**khūl**
Is there a swimming pool here?	هل يوجد حمام سباحة [بيسين] هنا ؟	hæl yūgæd ḥæm**mǣm** si**bǣ**ḥæ [pi**sīn**] **ho**nǣ
Is it open-air or indoors?	هل هو مكشوف أم مغطى ؟	hæl **ho**wæ mæk**shūf** æm mo**gat**tā
Is it heated?	هل هو مدفأ ؟	hæl **ho**wæa mo**dæf**fæ'
Can one swim in the lake/river?	هل يمكن الاستحمام فى البحيرة / النهر ؟	hæl **yom**kin æl 'istiḥ**mǣm** fil boḥ**æy**ra/æl nahr
I'd like to see a boxing/wrestling match.	أريد مشاهدة مباراة ملاكمة / مصارعة .	o**rid** moshǣ**hæ**dæt mobā**rāt** mo**læk**mæ/ mo**sar**'a
Can you get me 2 tickets?*	هل يمكنك شراء تذكرتين لى ؟	hæl yom**kin**æk shi**rā**' tæzkar**tēn** li

* see grammar

RELAXING

Is there a football (soccer) match anywhere this Friday?	هل توجد مباراة كرة قدم يوم الجمعة ؟	hæl **tū**gæd muba**rāt ko**rit **ka**dam yōm æl **go**maa
Who's playing?	من يلعب ؟	mæn **yæl**'æb
Is there any good fishing around here?	هل الصيد جيد هنا ؟	hæl æl sēd **gæ**yyid ho**nǣ**
Do I need a permit?	هل أنا محتاج لترخيص ؟	hæl æ**nǣ** moḥ**tǣg** litar**khīs**
Where can I get one?	أين يمكن الحصول على ترخيص ؟	æynæ **yom**kin æl ḥo**sūl** æ**lǣ** tar**khis**
Is there a bowling alley/billiard hall near here?	هل يوجد ملعب بولنج / بلياردو قريب ؟	hæl **yū**gæd **mæl**'æb **bō**ling/ bil**yar**do ka**rīb**

On the beach

Where's the beach?	أين الشاطىء ؟	æynæ æl **shā**ti'
Is it safe for swimming?	هل الاستحمام أمان ؟	hæl æl 'istiḥ**mǣm** 'æ**mǣn**
Is there a lifeguard?	هل يوجد غطاس ؟	hæl **yū**gæd gat**tās**
Is it safe for children?	هل هو أمان للأطفال ؟	hæl **ho**wæ 'æ**mān** lil'at**fāl**
It's very calm.	انه هادىء جداً .	in**næ**ho **hǣ**di' **gid**dæn
Is it a good place for snorkelling?	هل هو مكـان مناسب للغطس ؟	hæl **ho**wæ mæ**kǣn** mo**nǣ**sib lil gats
Are there dangerous currents?	هل توجد تيارات خطيرة ؟	hæl **tū**gæd tay**yā**rāt kha**tī**ra
What time is high/low tide?	متى المـد / الجزر ؟	**mæ**tæ æl mædd/æl gæzr
What's the temperature of the water?	ما درجة حرارة المياه ؟	mǣ **da**ragit ḥa**rā**rit æl mi**yǣh**
I want to hire a/an/some...	أريد تأجير ...	o**rīd** tæ'**gīr**
air mattress	مرتبة هواء	**mær**tæbit hæ**wæ'**
bathing hut	كابينة لخلع الملابس	ka**bī**næ likhæl'**il** mæ**lǣ**bis
bathing suit	مايوه	mæ**yō**

deck chair	كرسى بلاج قماش	**kor**si plæzh 'om**ǣsh**
skin-diving equipment	أدوات غطس	ædæ**wǣt** gats
sunshade	شمسية	shæm**si**yyæ
swimming belt	حزام نجاة [عوامة]	ḥi**zǣm** næ**gǣ** (æw**wǣ**mæ)
tent	خيمـة	**khē**mæ
water skis	أدوات انزلاق على الماء	ædæ**wǣt** inzi**lǣk** 'æ**lǣ** æl mǣ'
Where can I rent a...?	أين أستأجر ... ؟	æynæ æs**tæ**'gir
canoe	مركب	mærkib
motor boat	مركب بموتور [لنش]	mærkib bimo**tōr** [lænsh]
rowing boat	مركب بمقاديف	mærkib bi mæ'ǣ**dīf**
sailing boat	مركب شراعية	mærkib shira'**iy**yæ
What's the charge per hour?	بكم الساعة ؟	bi**kæm** æl **sǣ**'æ

شاطىء خاص	ممنوع الاستحمام
PRIVATE BEACH	NO BATHING

Winter sports

From about mid-December until about mid-May you can ski at several locations in Lebanon.

I want to hire a/some...	أريد استئجار ...	o**rīd** isti'gār
ski boots	بوط سكى	bōt skī
ski poles	عصى سكى	asā skī
skiing equipment	معدات سكى	mo'id**dǣt** skī
skis	سكى	skī
toboggan	زحليقة	zoḥ**lē**'æ

Camping—Countryside

A sunny climate makes camping possible all year round—particularly along the Mediterranean Coast. However, campsites and facilities are limited, so check with the tourist office before setting out on your own. You can also camp near a house or on private land, but get permission from the owner first. People will always be happy to help you, and if you're lucky they'll even invite you in to share their meal.

Can we camp here?	هل نستطيع أن نعسكر هنا ؟	hæl næstat**ī** æn no'**æs**kir hon**ǣ**
Where can one camp for the night?	أين نستطيع أن نعسكر الليلة ؟	æynæ nastat**ī** æn no'**æs**kir æl **lē**læ
Is there a camping site near here?	هل يوجد معسكر قريب من هنـا ؟	hæl **yū**gæd mo'**as**kar kar**ī**b min **hon**ǣ
Is there drinking water?	هل توجد مياه للشرب ؟	hæl **tū**gæd miy**ǣh** lil shorb
Are there shopping facilities on the site?	هل يوجد دكان فى المعسكر ؟	hæl **yū**gæd dokk**ǣn** fil mo'**as**kar
Are there showers/toilets?	هل يوجد دش / حمام ؟	hæl **yū**gæd doshsh/ ḥæmm**ǣm**
What's the charge per day...?	بكم الليلة ... ؟	bi**kæm** æl **lē**læ
per person	لشخص	li**shakhs**
for a car	لسيارة	lisæyy**ā**ra
for a tent	لخيمة	li**khē**mæ
Is there a youth hostel anywhere near here?	هل يوجد بيت شباب قريب ؟	hæl **yū**gæd bēt shæ**bǣb** kar**ī**b
Do you know anyone who can put us up for the night?	هل تعرف أحدا يقبل أن يسكننا عنده الليلة ؟	hæl **ta**arif æḥædæn **yak**bæl æn yosæk**ki**nonæ in**dæ**ho æl **lē**læ

FOR CAMPING EQUIPMENT, see page 107

ممنوع التخييم

CAMPING PROHIBITED

How far is it to...?	ما هى المسافة الى ... ؟	mæ **hiyæ** æl mæ**sæ**fæ ilæ
How far is the next village?	ما هى المسافة الى القرية القادمة ؟	mæ **hiyæ** æl mæ**sæ**fæ ilæ æl **kar**ya æl kā**di**mæ
Are we on the right road for...?	هل نحن على الطريق الصحيح الى ... ؟	hæl **næḥ**no æ**læ** æl ta**rīk** æl sa**ḥīḥ** ilæ
Where does this road lead to?	الى أين يؤدى هذا الطريق ؟	ilæ æynæ yo'**æd**di **hæ**zæ æl ta**rīk**
Can you show us on the map where we are?	أين نحن على الخريطة من فضلك ؟	æynæ **næḥ**no æ**læ** æl kha**rī**ta min **fad**lak

Landmarks

airfield	مطار	ma**tār**
bridge	كوبرى [جسر]	**kob**ri [zhisr]
building	مبنى	**mæb**næ
canal	قناة	ka**næ**
castle	قصر	kasr
cliff	حافة الجبل	**ḥæf**fit æl **gæ**bæl
copse	أعشاب	æ**æshæb**
crossroads	مفترق طرق [تقاطع]	mof**ta**rak **to**rok [ta**kā**to]
desert	صحراء	**saḥ**rā'
excavations	تنقيب عن الآثار	tan**kīb** æn æl ā**sār**
farm	عزبة	**'iz**ba
ferry	معدية	mi'æd**diy**yæ
field	حقل	ḥakl
footpath	سكة	**sik**kæ
hamlet	قرية	**kar**ya
hill	تل	tæll
house	بيت	bēt

inn	استراحة	istirāḥa
lake	بحيرة	boḥēra
mound	تـل	tæll
mountain	جبل	gæbæl
mountain range	سلسلة جبال	silsilit gibæ̅l
oasis	واحة	wæ̅ḥæ
path	سكة	sikkæ
plain	سهل	sæhl
plantation	مزرعة	mazraa
pool	بركة	birkæ
railway	خط سكة حديد	khatt sikkæ ḥædīd
river	نهر	nahr
road	طريق	tarīk
ruins	أطلال	atlāl
sand dunes	تلال رملية	tilæ̅l ramliyyæ
sea	بحر	baḥr
spring	منبع	mænbææ
tower	برج	borg
track	سكة	sikkæ
tree	شجرة	shagara
valley	وادى	wæ̅di
village	قرية	karya
wadi	وادى	wæ̅di
well	بئر	bi'r
wood	غابة	gæ̅bæ
What's the name of this place?	ما اسم هذا المكان ؟	mæ̅ ism **hæ̅**zæ æl mæ**kæ̅n**
How high is that mountain?	ما ارتفاع هذا الجبل ؟	mæ̅ irti**fæ̅'** **hæ̅**zæ æl **gæ**bæl

...and if you're tired of walking, you can always try hitch-hiking—though you may have to wait a long time for a lift.

Can you give me a lift to...?	من فضلك وصلنى الى ...	min **fad**lak was**sal**nī ilæ̅

Making friends

Introductions

Despite the language barrier, you'll have no problem in striking up a conversation with Arabs, especially when they realize that you're a foreigner. As a matter of fact, they'll probably start the conversation first. Arabs are eager to help foreigners, and they're curious to learn about your country and way of life. It's quite possible that a chance meeting with an Arab will soon lead to an invitation to meet his family at home. Do accept, as such spontaneous hospitality is sincere, and bring some sweets or flowers for the hostess.

Here are a few phrases to get you started.

How do you do? How are you?	ازيك [كيفك] ؟	izzæyyæk [**kī**fæk]
Very well, thank you.	بخير . الحمد لله .	bi**khēr**. ælḥæmdolill**ǣh**
How's life?	كيف الحال ؟	**kæy**fæl ḥǣl
Fine thanks. And you?	كويس شكراً . وأنت ؟	kwæyyis **shok**ran. wæ **in**tæ
May I introduce Miss...	أقدم لك الآنسة ...	o**kad**dim læk æl '**ǣ**nissæ
I'd like you to meet a friend of mine.	أحب أن تقابل صديقا لى .	o**ḥib** æn to**kā**bil sa**dī**kan li
Ali, this is...	يا على ، هذا ...	yǣ **ali** **hǣ**zæ
My name's...	اسمى ...	**is**mi
Glad to know you.	تشرفنا .	tæsha**rra**fna

Follow-up

How long have you been here?	منذ متى وأنت هنا ؟	monzo mætǣ wæ intæ hobǣ
We've been here a week.	نحن هنا منذ أسبوع .	næḥno honǣ monzo osbū

Is this your first visit?	هل هذه أول زيارة لك ؟	hæl hæzihi awwal ziyāra læk
No, we came here last year.	لا . أتينا السنة الماضية .	læ. ætæynæ æl sænæ æl mādiyæ
Are you enjoying your stay?	هل أنت مبسوط هنا ؟	hæl 'æntæ mabsūt honæ
Yes. I like ... very much.	نعم . . . تعجبني جداً .	næ'æm ... to'giboni giddæn
Are you on your own?	هل أنت وحدك ؟	hæl æntæ wæḥdæk
I'm with...	أنا مع ...	ænæ mææ
my wife	زوجتى	zæwgæti
my husband	زوجى	zæwgi
my family	أسرتى	osrati
my parents	والداى	wælidæy
some friends	أصحابى	'asḥābi
Where do you come from?	من أين تاتى ؟	min æynæ tæ'ti
What part of ... do you come from?	من أى مكان فى ... تاتى ؟	min ayy mækæn fi ... tæ'ti
I'm from...	أنا من ...	ænæ min
Where are you staying?	أين تسكن ؟	æynæ tæskon
I'm a student.	أنا طالب .	ænæ tālib
What are you studying?	ماذا تدرس ؟	mæzæ tædross
We're here on holiday.	نحن هنا فى اجازة [فرصة] .	næḥno honæ fi ægæzæ [forsa]
I'm here on a business trip.	أنا هنا لشغل .	ænæ honæ li shogl
What kind of business are you in?	ما ذا تشتغل ؟	mæzæ tæshtægil
I hope we'll see you again soon.	أرجو أن أراك مرة أخرى قريباً ان شاء الله .	argū æn arākæ marra okhrā karībæn 'in shæ'allāh
See you later/See you tomorrow.	الى اللقاء / أراك غداً .	ilæ æl likā'/arākæ gædæn

The weather

The Arabs don't talk about the weather as much as we do, but if you can't think of a better way to enter into conversation with someone, try...

What a lovely day!	انه يوم جميل .	innæho yōm gæ**mīl**
What awful weather!	الجو سيء [وحش] .	æl gæw **sæy**yi' [wiḥish]
Isn't it hot/cold today?	أليس الجو حاراً / بارداً اليوم ؟	æ**læy**sæ æl gæw ḥarr/bærd æl yōm
The wind is very strong.	الهواء شديد جداً .	æl hæ**wǣ'** shæ**dīd gid**dæn
What's the temperature outside?	ما درجة الحرارة بالخارج ؟	mǣ **da**ragit æl ḥa**rā**ra bil **khǣ**rig
What's the weather forecast?	ما هى التنبؤات الجوية ؟	mǣ **h**iyæ æl tænæbbo'**ǣt** æl gæw**wiy**yæ

Invitations

My wife and I would like you to dine with us on...	زوجتى وأنا نحب أن تتعشى معنا يوم ...	zæw**gæ**ti wæ æ**nǣ** no**ḥibb** æn tætæ'**æsh**shǣ **mæ**'æ-næ yōm
Can you come to dinner tomorrow night?	هل تستطيع أن تاتى للعشاء مساء الغد ؟	hæl tasta**tī** æn **tæ**'ti lil æ**shǣ'** mæ**sǣ'** æl gædd
Can you join us for a drink this evening?	هل تشاركنا فى مشروب مساء اليوم ؟	hæl tus**hǣrik**næ fī mash**rūb** mæ**sǣ'** æl yōm
There's a party. Are you coming?	هناك حفلة هل تاتى ؟	ho**nǣk ḥæ**flæ. hæl **tæ**'tī
That's very kind of you.	هذا لطيف جداً منك .	**hǣ**zæ la**tīf gid**dæn **min**kæ
Great, I'd love to come.	عظيم ، يسرنى أن أحضر .	a**zīm**. yæsor**ro**ni æn **aḥ**dar

FOR TEMPERATURE, see page 183

What time shall we come?	متى نأتى ؟	**mæ**tǣ **næ**'ti
May I bring a friend (male/female)?	هل يمكن أن يأتى صديقى / صديقتى ؟	hæl **yom**kin æn **yæ**'ti sadīki/sadi**ka**ti
I'm afraid we've got to go now.	نستأذن فى الرحيل .	næs**tæ**'zin fil ra**ḥil**
Next time you must come to visit us.	المرة القادمة يجب أن تأتى لزيارتنا .	æl **mar**ra æl kā**di**mæ **yæ**gib æn **tæ**'ti liziyā**ra**tinæ
Thank you very much for an enjoyable evening.	شكراً جزيلا على هذه السهرة الجميلة .	**shok**ran gæ**zī**læn 'ælæ **hǣ**zihi æl **sah**ra æl gæ**mī**læ
Thanks for the party. It was great.	شكراً على الحفلة . كانت عظيمة .	**shok**ran 'ælǣ æl **ḥæf**læ. **kǣ**næt azīma

Dating

Would you like a cigarette?	سيجارة ؟	sigāra
Have you got a light, please?	أريد أن أولــع من فضلك.	o**rīd** æn a**wæl**læ'æ min **fad**lak
Can I get you a drink?	هل أقدم لك كأساً ؟	hæl o**kad**dim **læ**ki **kæ**'sæn
Excuse me, could you please help me?	هل تساعدينى من فضلك ؟	hæl tosæ'i**dī**ni min **fad**lik
I'm lost. Can you show me the way to...?	أنا تائه . من فضلك أرشدينى الى . . .	æ**nǣ** **tǣ'ih**. min **fad**lik ærshi**dī**ni ilǣ
Are you waiting for someone?	هل تنتظرين أحداً ؟	hæl tantazi**rī**næ æḥædæn
Are you free this evening?	هل أنت فاضية مساء اليوم ؟	hæl **æn**ti **fad**yā mæ**sǣ'** æl yōm
Would you like to go out with me tonight?	هل تحبين الخروج معى الليلة ؟	hæl toḥib**bī**næ æl kho**rūg** **mæ'ī** æl **lē**læ

Would you like to go dancing?	هل تحبين الذهاب للرقص ؟	hæl toḥibbīnæ æl zihææb lil raks
I know a good discotheque/restaurant.	أعرف مرقصا/مطعماً جيداً .	æærif markas/mat'am gæyyid
Shall we go to the cinema (movies)?	هل نذهب الى السينما ؟	hæl næzhæb ilææ æl sinimææ
I'd love to, thank you.	نعم أحب ، شكراً .	nææm oḥibb shokran
Where shall we meet?	أين نتقابل ؟	æynæ nætækābæl
When shall I pick you up?	فى أى ساعة أمر عليك للخروج ؟	fi æyy sææ'æ æmorr ælæyki lil khorūg
I'll call for you at 8.	سأحضر الساعة ٨ .	sæ'aḥdar æl sææ'æ 8
May I take you home?	هل أوصلك الى منزلك ؟	hæl awassalik ilææ mænzilik
Can I see you again tomorrow?	هل نتقابل غداً ؟	hæl nætækābæl gædæn
Thank you, it's been a wonderful evening.	شكراً . كانت سهرة ممتازة .	shokran. kaænæt sahra momtææzæ
I've enjoyed myself tremendously.	أنا انبسطت جداً .	'ænææ inbasatt giddæn
What's your telephone number?	ما نمرة تليفونك ؟	mææ nimrit tilifōnik
Do you live with your family?	هل تسكنين مع أسرتك ؟	hæl tæskonīnæ mæ'æ osratik
Do you live alone?	هل تسكنين وحدك ؟	hæl tæskonīnæ wæḥdik
What time do you have to be back?	متى يجب أن تعودى الى المنزل ؟	mætææ yægib 'æn tæ'ūdi ilææ æl mæænzil

MAKING FRIENDS

Shopping guide

This shopping guide is designed to help you find what you want with ease, accuracy and speed. It features:

1. a list of all major shops, stores and services;
2. some general expressions required when shopping to allow you to be specific and selective;
3. full details of the shops and services most likely to concern you. Here you will find advice, alphabetical lists of items and conversion charts listed under the headings below.

		Page
Bookshop	books, magazines, newspapers, stationery	105
Camping	camping supplies	107
Chemist's (pharmacy)	medicine, first-aid, cosmetics, toilet articles	109
Clothing	clothes, shoes, accessories	113
Electrical appliances	radios, tape recorders, shavers, records	120
Hairdresser's	barber's, ladies' hairdresser, beauty salon	122
Jeweller's	jewellery, watches, watch repairs	124
Laundry–Dry cleaning	usual facilities	127
Photography	cameras, accessories, films, developing	128
Provisions	this is confined to basic items required for picnics	130
Souvenirs	souvenirs, gifts, fancy goods	
Tobacconist's	smoker's requisites	133

Advice

In Egypt and Jordan, stores are open from 8.30 a.m. to 12.30 p.m. and from 4 to 7 p.m., Monday to Thursday, and from 8.30 a.m. to 12.30 p.m. on Saturdays. Although some small shops remain open on Friday, offices and department stores are closed. On Sunday the large stores are shut, but all other activities continue normally. In Lebanon, hours vary according to the season: from November to May stores are open from 8.30 a.m. to 1 p.m. and from 3 to 6 p.m., Monday to Friday, and from 8.30 a.m. until 12.30 p.m. on Saturdays. During the summer months they're open on weekdays from 8 a.m. until 1 p.m. only and are closed on Saturdays and Sundays.

Souk means "market" in Arabic. It's composed of a maze of narrow, winding alleys where all kinds of tradesmen and artisans are grouped together.

In the *souk* you'll see all sorts of jewellers and artisans at work inlaying wood with enamel and ivory, engraving or hammering copper or making pottery. Antique dealers abound, and merchants sell fine rugs and brocades—all this in an atmosphere scented with sandalwood, cinnamon and musk.

If you are interested in antiques, with a little luck you might come across an ancient coin, a piece of Coptic cloth or a statuette dating back to the pharaohs. Be sure to demand a museum certificate guaranteeing the authenticity of any very old objects you buy.

Remember that selling and bargaining are Eastern customs not without a certain charm. As you browse through the *souk,* take your time, and don't hesitate to accept a cup of coffee or mint tea offered you by a merchant.

Shops, stores and services

Where's the nearest...?	أين أقرب ... ؟	æynæ **akrab**
antique shop	محل أنتيكات	mæ**ḥ**æll æntik**ǣt**
art gallery	معرض فنون	maa**rad** fon**ū**n
bakery	مخبز	**mækh**bæz
bank	بنك	bænk
barber's	حلاق	ḥæll**āk**
bazaar	بازار [سوق]	baz**ā**r [sūk]
beauty salon	صالون تجميل	sal**ō**n tæg**m**īl
bookshop	مكتبة	mæk**tæ**bæ
butcher	جزار [لحام]	gazz**ā**r [læḥ**ḥǣm**]
candy store	محل حلويات [ملبّس]	mæ**ḥ**æll ḥælæwiy**yǣt** [mil**æ**bbiss]
chemist's	أجزخانة [فرماشية]	ægzæ**khǣ**næ [færmæ**shiy**yæ]
clothing store	محل ملابس	mæ**ḥ**æll mæl**ǣ**bis
cobbler	جزمجى [كندرجى]	gæzm**æ**gi [kin**darz**hi]
dairy	محل ألبان	mæ**ḥ**ill æl**bǣn**
dentist	طبيب أسنان	**tabib** æs**nǣn**
department store	محل كبير	mæ**ḥ**æll kæ**bir**
doctor	دكتور	dok**tō**r
dressmaker	خياطة	khay**yā**ta
drugstore	أجزخانة [فرماشية]	ægzæ**khǣ**næ [færmæ**shiy**yæ]
dry cleaner	محل تنظيف ملابس	mæ**ḥ**æll tan**zīf** mæl**ǣ**bis
fishmonger	محل سمك	mæ**ḥ**æll **sæ**mækk
florist	محل زهور	mæ**ḥ**æll zo**hūr**
furrier	محل فرو	mæ**ḥ**æll **far**rw
greengrocer	خضرى	**kho**dari
grocery	بقال	bak**kāl**
hairdresser's (ladies)	صالون تجميل	sal**ō**n tæg**m**īl
hardware store	محل أدوات منزلية	mæ**ḥ**æll ædæ**wǣt** mæn**ziliy**yæ
hat shop	محل برانيط	mæ**ḥ**æll bara**nit**

hospital	مستشفى	mostæshfǣ
ironmonger	محل أدوات منزلية	mæḥæll ædæwǣt mænziliyyæ
jeweller	جواهرجى	gæwæhirgi
laundry	غسيل ومكوة	gæsīl wæ mækwæ
leather-goods store	محل مصنوعات جلدية	mæḥæll masnū'āt gildiyyæ
market	سوق	sūk
milliner	صانعة برانيط	sāni'æt baranīt
newsagent	بائع جرائد	bǣ'i' garā'id
newsstand	كشك جرائد	koshk garā' id
optician	محل نظارات [عوينات]	mæḥæll nazzarāt [owæynǣt]
pastry shop	حلوانى	ḥælæwǣni
perfumery	محل عطور	mæḥæll otūr
photographer	مصور	mosawwir
photo shop	محل تصوير	mæḥæll taswīr
police station	قسم بوليس	kism bolīs
post office	مكتب بريد	mæktæb bærīd
shoemaker (repairs)	جزمجى [كندرجى]	gæzmægi [kindarzhi]
shoe shop	محل جزم [أحذية]	mæḥæll gizæm [æḥziyæ]
souvenir shop	محل سوفنير	mæḥæll sūvinīr
sporting goods shop	محل أدوات رياضية	mæḥæll ædæwǣt riyāddiyya
stationer	مكتبة	mæktæbæ
supermarket	سوبر ماركت	sūpir markit
sweet shop	محل حلويات [ملبس]	mæḥæll ḥælæwiyyǣt [milæbbis]
tailor	ترزى [خياط]	tærzi [khayyāt]
tobacconist	محل سجاير [دخان]	mæḥæll sægǣyir [dokhkhǣn]
travel agent	مكتب سياحى	mæktæb siyǣḥi
vegetable store	خضرى	khodari
veterinarian	طبيب بيطرى	tabīb bitari
watchmaker	محل ساعات	mæḥæll sæǣt

General expressions

Here are some expressions which will be useful to you when you're out shopping.

Where?

Where's a good...?	أين يوجد ... جيد ؟	æynæ yūgæd...gæyyid
Where can I find a...?	أين أجد ... ؟	æynæ ægid
Where do they sell...?	أين يباع ... ؟	æynæ yobæ'
Can you recommend an inexpensive...?	هل يمكنك أن تنصحنى بـ... رخيص ؟	hæl yomkinæk æn tænsaḥni bi...rakhīs
Where's the main shopping area?	أين مركز المحلات الرئيسى ؟	æynæ mærkæz æl mæḥillæt æl ra'īssi
How far is it from here?	ما بعده عن هنا ؟	mæ bo'doh æn honæ
How do I get there?	كيف أصل اليه ؟	kæyfæ asil ilæyhi

Service

Can you help me?	هل يمكنك مساعدتى ؟	hæl yomkinæk mosæ'ædæti
I'm just looking around.	اننى أتفرج فقط .	innæni ætæfarrag fakatt
I want...	أريد . . .	orīd
Can you show me some...?	هل يمكنك أن ترينى ... ؟	hæl yomkinæk æn torīni
Have you any...?	هل عندك ... ؟	hæl indæk

That one

Can you show me that one?	من فضلك أرينى هذا .	min fadlak ærīni hæzæ
It's over there.	انه هناك .	innæho honæk

Defining the article

I want a ... one.	أريد شيئاً ...	orīd shæy'æn
big	كبير	kæbīr
coloured	ملون	molæwwæn
dark	غامق	gǣmik
good	جيد	gæyyid
heavy	ثقيل	ti'īl
large	كبير	kæbīr
light (weight)	خفيف	khæfīf
light (colour)	فاتح	fǣtiḥ
long	طويل	tawīl
round	مستدير	mostædīr
short	قصير	kasīr
small	صغير	sagīr
square	مربع	morabbaa
I don't want anything too expensive.	لا أريد شيئاً غاليا .	lǣ orīd shæy'æn gǣliyæn

Preference

Can you show me some more?	أريد أن أرى شيئاً آخراً من فضلك .	orīd æn arā shæy'æn ākhar min fadlak
Haven't you anything...?	هل عندك شيء ... ؟	hæl indæk shē'
cheaper/better	أرخص / أحسن	arkhas/æḥsæn
larger/smaller	أكبر / أصغر	akbar/asgar

How much?

How much is this?	بكم هذا ؟	bikæm hǣzæ
I don't understand. Please write it down.	لا أفهم . من فضلك أكتب لى الثمن .	lǣ æfhæm. min fadlak iktib li æl tæmæn
I don't want to spend more than...	لا أريد أن أدفع أكثر من ...	lǣ orīd æn ædfææ aktar min

FOR NUMBERS, see page 175

Decision

That's just what I want.	هذا هو المطلوب .	hǣzæ howæl matlūb
No, I don't like it.	لا . لا تعجبنى .	lǣ. lǣ to'giboni
I'll take it.	سآخذها .	sæ'ǣkhodhæ

Ordering

Can you order it for me?	هـل يمكنك أن توصى عليها لى ؟	hæl yomkinæk æn towassi ælæyhǣ li
How long will it take?	متى تكون جاهزة ؟	mætǣ tækūn gǣhizæ

Delivery

I'll take it with me.	سآخذها معى .	sæ'ǣkhodhæ mæ'i
Deliver it to the ... hotel.	وصلها الى فندق ...	wassilhǣ ilæ fondok
Please send it to this address.	من فضلك أرسلها الى هذا العنوان .	min fadlak ærsilhǣ ilǣ hǣzæl 'inwǣn
Will I have any difficulty with the customs?	هل سأجد صعوبة فى الجمرك؟	hæl sæ'ægid so'ūba fil gomrok

Paying

How much is it?	بكم ؟	bikæm
Can I pay by traveller's cheque?	هل يمكن الدفع بشيكات سياحية ؟	hæl yomkin æl dæf' bishēkǣt siyǣḥiyyæ
Do you accept dollars/pounds/credit cards?	هل تقبـل الدولارات / الجنيهات / بطاقات الرصيد ؟	hæl takbal æl dōlārāt/æl gonæyhǣt/bitākāt æl rasīd
Haven't you made a mistake in the bill?	ألا توجد غلطة فى الفاتورة ؟	'ælǣ tūgæd galta fil fatūra
Can I have a receipt, please?	أريد فاتورة [ايصال] من فضلك .	orīd fatūra ['īsāl] min fadlak

Anything else?

No, thanks, that's all.	لا ، شكرا . يكفى هذا .	lǣ **shokran**. yækfi **hǣ**zæ
Yes, I want...	نعم ، أريد ...	**næ**æm. o**rīd**
Thank you. Good-bye.	شكرا . مع السلامة .	**shok**ran. maassæ**lǣ**mæ

Dissatisfied

Can you please exchange this?	هل يمكنك تغيير هذا من فضلك ؟	hæl yom**ki**næk tæg**yīr** **hǣ**zæ min **fad**lak
I want to return this.	أريد ارجاع هذا .	o**rīd** ir**gǣ**' **hǣ**zæ
I'd like a refund.	أريد استرداد الثمن .	o**rīd** istir**dǣd** æl **tæ**mæn
Here's the receipt.	هذا هو الايصال .	**hǣ**zæ **ho**wæl 'i**sāl**

هل استطيع مساعدتك ؟	Can I help you?
أى ... تريد ؟	What ... would you like?
لون / شكل	colour/shape
نوع / كمية	quality/quantity
آسف . ليس عندى منه .	I'm sorry, we haven't any.
لقد انتهى ما كان عندنا منه.	We're out of stock.
هل نوصى لك عليه ؟	Shall we order it for you?
هل تاخذه معك أم يجب أن نرسله لك ؟	Will you take it with you or shall we send it?
أى شىء آخر ؟	Anything else?
... (الثمن) من فضلك .	That's ... please.
لا نقبل ...	We don't accept...
بطاقات الرصيد	credit cards
الشيكات السياحية	traveller's cheques
الشيكات الخاصة	personal cheques

Bookshop—Stationer's—Newsstand

In the Middle East, bookshops and stationers may be combined or separate. Newspapers and magazines may be sold in bookshops, in kiosks or at the stationer's.

Where's the nearest…?	أين أقرب … ؟	æynæ akrab
bookshop	مكتبة	mæktæbæ
stationer's	محل أدوات كتابة	mæḥæll ædæwǣt kitǣbæ
newsstand	كشك جرائد	koshk garā'id
I want to buy a/an/ some…	أريد شراء …	orīd shirā'
address book	دفتر عناوين	daftar ænæwīn
ball-point pen	قلم حبر جاف	kalam ḥibr gǣf
book	كتاب	kitǣb
box of paints	علبة ألوان	ilbit ælwǣn
carbon paper	ورق كربون	warak karbōn
cellophane tape	شريط لاصق	shirīt lāsik
crayons	أقلام ألوان	aklām ælwǣn
dictionary	قاموس	kamūs
Arabic–English	عربى – انجليزى	arabi-ingilīzi
English–Arabic	انجليزى – عربى	ingilīsi-arabi
pocket dictionary	قاموس للجيب	kamūs lil gēb
drawing paper	ورق رسم	warak ræsm
drawing pins	دبابيس رسم	dæbæbis ræsm
envelopes	ظروف	zorūf
eraser	أستيكة [ممحاة]	æstikæ [mimḥǣh]
fountain pen	قلم حبر	kalam ḥibr
glue	صمغ	samg
grammar book	كتاب نحو	kitǣb næḥw
guide book	دليل سياحى	dælīl siyǣḥi
ink	حبر	ḥibr
black/red/blue	أسود/أحمر/أزرق	æswæd/aḥmar/æzrak

SHOPPING GUIDE

labels	بطاقات	bitā**kāt**
magazine	مجلة	mæ**g**æ**ll**æ
map	خريطة	kharīta
map of the town	خريطة للمدينة	kharīta lil mædīnæ
road map	خريطة للطرق	kharīta lil torok
newspaper	جريدة	gærīdæ
American/English	أمريكانى / انجليزى	æmrikǣni/ingilīzi
notebook	مفكرة [بلوك نوت]	mofækkira [blok-nōt]
note paper	ورق خطابات	warak khitabāt
paperback	كتاب جيب	kitǣb gēb
paper napkins	فوط ورق	fowatt warak
pen	قلم حبر	kalam ḥibr
pencil	قلم رصاص	kalam rosās
pencil sharpener	برّاية	bærrǣyæ
playing cards	ورق لعب [كوتشينة]	warak liib [kotshīnæ]
postcards	كروت بوستال	korūt postāl
refill (for a pen)	أنبوبة حبر جاف	onbūbit ḥibr gǣf
rubber	أستيكة [ممحاة]	æstīkæ [mimḥæh]
rubber bands	أستيـــك	æstik
ruler	مسطرة	mastara
sketching block	كراس سكتش	korrās skitch
stamps	طوابع بريد	tawābi' bærīd
string	خيط [دوبار]	khēt [dobār]
thumb tacks	دبابيس رسم	dæbæbīs ræsm
tissue paper	ورق كلينكس	warak klīniks
typewriter ribbon	شريط لآلة كاتبة	shirīt li'ǣlæ kǣtbæ
typing paper	ورق لآلة كاتبة	warak li'ǣlæ kǣtbæ
wrapping paper	ورق لف	warak læff
writing pad	بلوك ورق	blok warak
Where's the guide-book section?	أين قسم «الدليل السياحى»؟	æynæ kism "æl dælīl æl siyǣhi"
Where do you keep the English books?	أين قسم الكتب الانجليزية ؟	æynæ kism æl kotob æl 'ingiliziyyæ

Camping

I'd like a/an/some...	أريد ...	**orīd**
axe	بالطة	**bal**ta
bottle-opener	فتاحة زجاجات	fætt**ǣ**ḥit zogæ**gǣt**
bucket	جردل [سطل]	**gær**dæl [satl]
butane gas	أنبوبة بوتاجاز	onb**ū**bit botæ**gǣz**
camp cot	سرير للسفر	si**rīr** lil **sa**far
camping equipment	معدات تخييم	mo'id**dǣt** tæk**hyīm**
can opener	فتاحة علب	fætt**ǣ**ḥit 'ilæb
candles	شمع	shæm'
(folding) chair	كرسى (بلاج)	**kor**si (pl**ǣ**zh)
compass	برجل [بيكار]	**bær**gæl [bi**kār**]
corkscrew	بـرِّيمة لفتح الزجاجات	bær**rī**mæ li**fæt**ḥ æl zogæ**gǣt**
crockery	أطباق	at**bāk**
cutlery	فضية	fad**diy**yæ
first-aid kit	علبة اسعافات أولية	ilbitt is'**ǣ**f**ǣt** æwwæ**liy**yæ
flashlight	بطـارية	battā**riy**yæ
frying pan	طاسة	**tā**sa
groundsheet	خيمة	**khē**mæ
hammer	شاكوش	shæ**kūsh**
hammock	سرير معلق	si**rīr** mo'**al**lak
ice-bag	كيس ثلج	kis tælg
kerosene	كيروسين	kiro**sīn**
kettle	غلاية	gæll**ǣ**yæ
lamp	لمبة	**lam**ba
lantern	مصباح	mis**bāḥ**
matches	كبريت [شحيطة]	kæb**rīt** [shaḥ**ḥē**ta]
mattress	مرتبة	**mær**tæbæ
methylated spirits	كحول	ko**ḥoll**
mosquito net	ناموسية	næmū**siy**yæ
paraffin	كيروسين	kiro**sīn**
penknife	مطوة	**mat**wa

picnic case	صندوق للرحلات	**sondūk** lil **riḥlæt**
primus stove	وابور جاز	**wabūr** gæz
rope	حبل	ḥæbl
rucksack	شنطة للظهر	**shanta** lil dahr
saucepan	حلة	ḥællæ
screwdriver	مفك	**mifækk**
sheathknife	مطوة	**matwa**
sleeping bag	كيس للنوم	kīs lil nōm
stove	فرن	forn
(folding) table	ترابيزة [طاولة] (للبلاج)	tarabēza [tawla] (lil plæzh)
tent	خيمة	**khēmæ**
tent pegs	أوتاد خيمة	æwtæd khēmæ
tent poles	عواميد خيمة	æwæmīd khēmæ
thermos flask (bottle)	ترموس	**tirmos**
tin opener	فتاحة علب	fættæḥit 'ilæb
tongs	زرادية	zarradiyyæ
torch	بطارية	battāriyya
water carrier	حامل للماء	ḥæmil lilmæh'
wood alcohol	كحول	**koḥoll**

Crockery

cups	فناجيل	fænægīl
food box	علبة طعام	**ilbit taām**
plates	أطباق	**atbāk**
saucers	أطباق للفرن	atbāk lil forn

Cutlery

forks	شوك	**showæk**
knives	سكاكين	sækækīn
spoons	ملاعق	mælæik
(made of) plastic	بلاستيك	**plastik**
(made of) stainless steel	معدنية	mæ'dæniyyæ

Chemist's (drugstore)

In the Middle East, chemists normally don't stock the great range of goods that you'll find in England or the U.S. In the window you'll see a notice telling you where the nearest all-night chemist's is.

For reading ease, this section has been divided into two parts:

1. Pharmaceutical—medicine, first-aid, etc.
2. Toiletry—toilet articles, cosmetics.

General

Where's the nearest chemist's?	أين أقرب أجزخـانة [فرماشية] ؟	æynæ **akrab** ægzæ**khæ**næ [fær**mæshiyyæ**]
What time does the chemist open/close?	متى تفتح / تقفل الاجزخانة [الفرماشية] ؟	**mætæ tæftæḥ/takfil** æl ʻægzæ**khæ**næ [æl færmæ**shiyyæ**]

Part 1—Pharmaceutical

I want something for…	أريد شيئا لـ ...	orīd **shæy**ʼæn li
Can you recommend something for…?	هل يمكنك أن تنصحنى بشىء لـ ... ؟	hæl yomkinæk æn tæn**saḥ**nī bi **shæy**ʼin li
a cold/a cough	برد / سعال	bærd/so**æl**
a hangover	دوخة	**dō**khæ
sunburn	ضربة شمس	**dar**bit shæms
travel sickness	دوار السفر	dow**ār** ælsafar
Can you make up this prescription?	هل يمكنك أن تجهز لى هذه الروشيتة ؟	hæl yomkinæk æn to**gæ**hhiz li **hæ**zihi æl **roshit**tæ
Shall I wait?	هل أنتظر ؟	hæl **antazir**
When shall I come back?	متى أرجع ؟	**mætæ argaa**

FOR DOCTORS, see page 162

Can I get it without a prescription?	هل يباع بلا روشيتة ؟	hæl yobææ bilæ roshittæ
Can I have a/an/ some...?	أريد ...	orīd
antiseptic cream	كريم مطهر	krēm motahhir
Band-Aids	شريط لاصق	shirīt lāsik
bandage	رباط ـ شاش	robāt-shæsh
chlorine tablets	حبوب كلور	ḥobūb klōr
corn plasters	شريط للكالو	shirīt lil kallo
cotton wool	قطن طبى	kotn tibbī
cough drops	نقط للسعلة	no'at lil sæælæ
diabetic lozenges	سكارين	sækærīn
disinfectant	مطهر	motahhir
ear drops	نقط للاذن	no'at lil 'ozon
Elastoplast	شريط لاصق	shirīt lāsik
eye drops	قطرة للعيون	katra lil oyūn
flea powder	بودرة للبراغيث	bodra lil bæræghīt
gargle	غرغرة	gargara
gauze	شاش	shæsh
insect lotion	لوسيون ضد الحشرات	losyōn did æl ḥasharāt
insect repellent	طارد للحشرات	tārid lil ḥasharāt
iodine	يــود	yōd
laxative	ملين	molæyyin
mouthwash	غسيل للفم	gæsīl lil fæm
quinine tablets	أقراص كينين	akrās kinīn
sanitary napkins	فوط ورق طبى	fowatt warak tibbi
sleeping pills	حبوب منومة	ḥobūb monæwwimæ
stomach pills	أقراص للهضم	akrās lil hadm
thermometer	ترمومتر	tirmomitr
throat lozenges	أقراص للزور	akrās lil zōr
tissues	غيارات	giyarāt
tranquillizers	أقراص مهدئة	akrās mohæddi'æ
vitamin pills	أقراص فيتامين	akrās vitæmīn

Part 2—Toiletry

I'd like a/an/some...	أريد ...	**orīd**
acne cream	كريم لحب الشباب	krēm li**ḥæbb** æl shæ**bæb**
after-shave lotion	لوسيون بعد الحلاقة	los**yōn baad** æl ḥi**lā**ka
astringent	قابض	**kā**bid
bath salts	أملاح للحمام	æm**læḥ** lil ḥæm**mæm**
cologne	كلونيا	kolonyæ
cream	كريم	krēm
cleansing cream	كريم للتنظيف	krēm lil tanzīf
cold cream	كولد كريم	kold krēm
cuticle cream	كريم لسطح الجلد	krēm li saṭḥ æl gild
foundation cream	كريم أساسى	krēm æ**sæ**si
moisturizing cream	كريم مرطب	krēm **moratt**ib
night cream	كريم لليل	krēm lil lēl
deodorant	مزيل لرائحة العرق	mozīl li rā'iḥæt æl 'arak
emery board	مبرد أظافر كرتون	**mabrad** azāfir kar**tōn**
eye pencil	قلم كحل للعين	**ka**lam koḥl lil ēn
eye shadow	ظل للعيون	zill lil **oyūn**
face flannel	فوطة لتنظيف الوجه	**fū**ta litanzīf æl wægh
face powder	بودرة للوجه	**bod**ra lil wægh
foot cream/powder	كريم / بودرة للقدم	krēm/**bod**ra lil **ka**dam
hand cream/lotion	كريم / لوسيون لليد	krēm/los**yōn** lil yædd
Kleenex	كلينكس	**klī**niks
lipsalve	ملون للشفايف	mo**læw**win lil shæ**fæ**yif
lipstick	روج للشفايف	rūzh lil shæ**fæ**yif
make-up remover pads	قصائص مزيلة للتواليت	kasā'is mozīlæ lil **twælitt**
mascara	كحل	koḥl
nail brush	فرشاة للاظافر	**for**shæ lil azāfir
nail clippers	أصافة للاظافر	'as**sā**fa lil azāfir
nail file	مبرد أظافر	**mabrad** azāfir
nail polish	ملمع للاظافر	mo**læm**mi' lil 'azāfir
nail polish remover	مزيل للون الاظافر	mozīl li**lōn** æl 'azāfir

SHOPPING GUIDE

nail scissors	مقص للاظافر	makass lil azāfir
oil	زيت	zēt
perfume	عطر	itr
powder	بودرة	bodra
powder puff	بخاخة بودرة	bækhkhæækhit bodra
razor blades	أمواس حلاقة	æmwææs ḥilææka
rouge	أحمر شفاة	aḥmar shifææh
shampoo	شامبو	shæmpū
shaving brush	فرشاة للحلاقة	forshæ lil ḥilææka
shaving cream	كريم للحلاقة	krēm lil ḥilææka
shaving soap	صابون للحلاقة	sabūn lil ḥilææka
soap	صابون	sabūn
sponge	سفنجة	sæfingæ
sun-tan cream/oil	كريم / زيت للشمس	krēm/zēt lil shæms
talcum powder	بودرة تلك	bodra tælk
toilet paper	ورق تواليت	warak twælitt
toilet water	ماء للتواليت	mææ' lil twælitt
toothbrush	فرشاة للاسنان	forshæ lil æsnææn
toothpaste	معجون للاسنان	mææægūn lil æsnææn
towel	فوطة	fūta
wash cloth	فوطة لتنظيف الوجه	fūta litanzīf æl wægh

For your hair

brush	فرشاة	forshæ
colouring	صبغة	sabga
comb	مشط	misht
curlers	لفائف للتمويج	læfææ'if lil tæmwīg
grips	ماسكات [بنس]	mæsikææt [binæss]
lacquer	حافظ التسريحة (لاكيه)	ḥāfiz æl tæsrīḥæ (lækēh)
(bobby) pins	دبابيس للشعر	dæbæbīs lil shaar
setting lotion	سائل للتسريح	sææ'il lil tæsrīḥ

Clothing

If you want to buy something specific, prepare yourself in advance. Look at the list of clothing on page 118. Get some idea of the colour, material and size you want. They're all listed in the next few pages.

General

'd like…	أريد ...	orīd
want … for a 10-ear-old boy/girl.	أريد ... لولد / لبنت عمره ١٠ سنوات .	orīd…liwælæd/libint omro 10 sænæwææt
want something like his.	أريد شيئاً مثل هذا .	orīd shæy'æn misl hææzæ
like the one in the window.	يعجبنى ما فى الفيترينة .	yo'giboni mææ fil vitrīnæ
How much is that per metre?	بكم المتر من هذا ؟	bikæm æl mitr min hææzæ

1 centimetre	= 0.39 in.	1 inch	= 2.54 cm.
1 metre	= 39.37 in.	1 foot	= 30.5 cm.
10 metres	= 32.81 ft.	1 yard	= 0.91 m.

Colour

want something n…	أريد لون ...	orīd lōn
want a darker/lighter shade.	أريده أغمق / أفتح .	orīd ægmak/æftæḥ
want something to match this.	أريد شيئاً يناسب هذا .	orīd shæy'æn yonæsib hææzæ
don't like the colour.	لا يعجبنى اللون .	lææ yo'giboni æl lōn

beige	بيج	bēzh
black	أسود	æswæd
blue	أزرق	æzrak
brown	بنى	bonnī
cream	كريم	krēm
emerald	أخضر زمردى	akhdarr zomorrodī
golden	ذهبى	zæhæbī
green	أخضر	akhdarr
grey	رمادى	romādī
orange	برتقالى	bortokālī
pink	وردى	wærdī
purple	بنفسجى	bænæfsigī
red	أحمر	aḥmar
scarlet	أحمر غامق [نبيذى]	aḥmar gǣmik [nibītī]
silver	فضى	faddī
white	أبيض	abyad
yellow	أصفر	asfar

مخطط
(mokhattat)

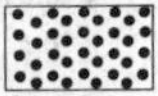
منقط
(monakkat)

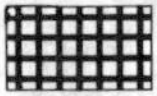
مربعات
(morabbaāt)

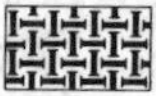
مزركش
(mozarkash)

Material

Have you anything in...?	هل عندك قماش ... ؟	hæl indæk komāsh
Is that...?	هل هذا ... ؟	hæl hǣzæ
hand-embroidered	مشغول باليد	mæshgūl bil yæd
hand-made	شغل يد	shogl yæd
made here	مصنوع هنا	masnū honǣ

What's it made of?

brocade	بروكار	brokār
cambric	تيل خفيف	tīl khæfīf
camel hair	وبر الجمل	wabar gæmæl
chiffon	شيفون	shifōn
corduroy	قطيفة مضلعة	katīfa modallaa
cotton	قطن	kotn
damask	دماسيه	dæmæsē
felt	جوخ	gūkh
flannel	فانلة	fænillæ
gabardine	جبردين	gæbærdīn
lace	دانتيل	dæntillæ
leather	جلد	gild
linen	كتان [تيل]	kittǣn [tīl]
pique	قطن	kotn
poplin	بوبلين	poplīn
rayon	حرير صناعى	ḥærīr sinā'ī
rubber	كاوتش	kæwitch
silk	حرير	ḥærīr
suede	شاموا	shæmwā
taffeta	تفتاه	tæftæ
terrycloth	قماش مسامى	omǣsh mæsǣmi
velvet	قطيفة	katīfa
wool	صوف	sūf

Size

I take size...	مقاسى ...	makāsī
Could you measure me?	هل يمكن أن تقيس لى ؟	hæl yomkin æn takīs lī
I don't know your sizes.	لا أعرف مقاساتكم .	lǣ aarif makasatkom

In that case, look at the charts on the next page.

This is your size

Ladies

Dresses/Suits						
US	10	12	14	16	18	20
Britain	32	34	36	38	40	42
Middle East	42	44	46	48	50	52

Stockings		Shoes			
US	sizes are the same	6	7	8	9
Britain		4	5	6	7
Middle East		37	38	40	41

Gentlemen

	Suits/Overcoats						Shirts			
US / Britain	36	38	40	42	44	46	15	16	17	18
Middle East	46	48	50	52	54	56	38	41	43	45

Shoes									
US / Britain	5	6	7	8	8	9	9	10	11
Middle East	38	39	41	42	43	43	44	44	45

Sizes may vary somewhat from country to country, so the above must be taken as an approximate guide.

A good fit?

Can I try this on?	هل يمكن أن أقيس هذا ؟	hæl **yomkin** æn akīs **hǣ**zæ
Where's the fitting room?	أين حجرة القياس ؟	æynæ **ḥog**rat æl kiyǣs
Is there a mirror?	هل توجد مراية ؟	hæl **tū**gæd mir**ǣ**yæ

FOR NUMBERS, see page 175

It fits very well.	المقاس مضبوط جدا .	æl makās madbūt giddæn
It doesn't fit.	المقاس ليس مضبوطاً .	æl makās læysæ madbūt
It's too...	انه ... جداً ...	innæho...giddæn
short/long	قصير / طويل	kasir/tawīl
tight/loose	ضيق / واسع	dayyik/wææsii
How long will it take to alter?	متى ينتهى التصليح ؟	mætæ yæntæhi æl taslīḥ

Shoes

I'd like a pair of...	أريد ...	orīd
shoes/sandals/boots	حذاء / صندل / بوط	ḥizææ'/sandal/bōt
These are too...	انه ... جداً	innæho...giddæn
narrow/wide	ضيق / واسع	dayyik/wææsii
large/small	كبير / صغير	kæbīr/sagīr
Do you have a larger size?	هل عندك مقاس أكبر ؟	hæl indæk makās akbar
I want a smaller size.	أريد مقاس أصغر .	orīd makās asgar
Do you have the same in...?	هل عندك لون ...	hæl indæk lōn
brown/beige	بنى / بيج	bonni/bēzh
black/white	أسود / أبيض	æswæd/abyad

Shoes worn out? Here's the key to getting them fixed again...

Can you repair these shoes?	هل يمكنك اصلاح هذا الحذاء ؟	hæl yomkinæk islāḥ hææzæ æl ḥizææ'
Can you stitch this?	هل يمكنك تخييط هذا ؟	hæl yomkinæk takhyīt hææzæ
I want new soles and heels.	أريد نعل و كعب جديدين .	orīd nææl wæ kæææb gædidēn
When will they be ready?	متى تكون جاهزة ؟	mætæ tækūn gæhzæ

SHOPPING GUIDE

Clothes and accessories

I'd like a/an/some...	أريد ...	**orīd**
bath robe	برنس	**bornos**
bathing cap	بونيه للبحر	bon**ē** lil ba**ḥ**r
bathing suit	بدلة بحر [مايوه]	**bæd**lit ba**ḥ**r [mæ**yō**]
blazer	جاكته بليزر	zhæ**kit**tæ **blē**zær
blouse	قميص حريمي	a**mīs** ḥæ**rī**mī
boots	بوط	bōt
bow tie	كرافاته بابيون	kara**vat**ta pap**yōn**
bra	حامل صدر [سوتيان]	**ḥæ**mil sadr [sūt**yæn**]
braces (Br.)	حمالات	hæmmæ**læt**
briefs	لباسات [شناتين]	libæ**sæt** [shnæ**tīn**]
cap	كاسكتة	kæs**kit**tæ
cape	كابة [حرملة]	**kæ**bæ [**ḥar**mala]
coat	معطف	**mi'**taf
costume	بدلة	**bæd**læ
dinner jacket	بدلة سموكنج	**bæd**læ **smō**king
dress	فستان	fos**tæn**
dressing gown	روب	**rōb**
evening dress	فستان للسهرة	fos**tæn** lil **sah**ra
fur coat	معطف فرو	**mi'**taf farw
girdle	حزام	ḥi**zæm**
gloves	جوانتي [كفوف]	go**wæn**ti [kfūf]
handkerchief	منديل	mæn**dīl**
hat	قبعة	kob**baa**
jacket	جاكتة	zhæ**kit**tæ
jeans	بنطلون «بلوجين»	banta**lōn** blū zhinz
jersey	بلوفر	po**lō**var
jumper (Br.)	بلوفر	po**lō**var
nightdress	قميص نوم	ka**mīs** nōm
panty-girdle	كورسيه	kor**sē**
panty hose	شراب حريمي طويل	sho**rāb** ḥæ**rī**mī ta**wīl**

pyjamas	بيجامة	pizhǣmæ
raincoat	معطف مطر	mi'taf matar
sandals	صندل	sandal
scarf	اشارب	isharp
shirt	قميص	kamīs
shoes	حذاء [سباط]	ḥizǣ' [sobbāt]
shorts (Br.)	شورت	short
skirt	جوب	jūp
socks	شراب [كالسات]	shorāb [kælsǣt]
stockings	شراب حريمى	shorāb ḥærīmi
suit (man's)	بدلة	bædlæ
suit (woman's)	فستان	fostǣn
suspenders	حمالة	ḥæmmǣlæ
sweater	جاكتة	zhækittæ
tennis shoes	حذاء رياضى	ḥizǣ' riyādi
tie	كرافات	kravāt
tights	شراب حريمى طويل	shorāb ḥærīmi tawīl
trousers	بنطلون	bantalōn
underpants (men)	لباسات [شناتين]	libæsǣt [shnætīn]
undershirt	فانلة	fænillæ
vest (Am.)	صديرى	sidēri
vest (Br.)	فانلة	fænillæ
waistcoat	صديرى	sidēri

belt	حزام	ḥizǣm
buckle	توكة	tōkæ
button	زرار	zorār
collar	ياقة	yǣka
pocket	جيب	gēb
shoe laces	رباط أحذية	robāt æḥziyæ
zip (zipper)	سوستة	sostæ

Electrical appliances and accessories—Records

There is no standard voltage within any single Middle-Eastern country, let alone throughout the region as a whole. The voltages are, in general: 110–220 volts AC, 50 cycles in Egypt (220 volts in central Cairo); 220 volts AC, 50 cycles in Jordan; and 110 volts AC, 50 cycles in Lebanon. So check before you plug your appliance in. The plug in use throughout the Middle East is the two-round-pin type.

What's the voltage?	كم الفولت ؟	kæm æl volt
I want a plug for this.	أريد بريزة لهذا .	orīd prīzæ lihǣzæ
Do you have a battery for this.	هل عندك بطارية لهذا ؟	hæl indæk battāriyyæ lihǣzæ
This is broken. Can you repair it?	هذا مكسور . هل يمكنك اصلاحه ؟	hǣzæ mæksūr. hæl yomkinæk islāḥoh
When will it be ready?	متى يكون جاهزاً ؟	mǣtǣ yækūn gǣhizæn
I'd like a/an/some...	أريد ...	orīd
adapter	بريزة أمريكانى	prīzæ æmrikǣni
battery	بطارية	battāriyyæ
blender	خلاط	khallāt
food mixer	خلاط	khallāt
hair dryer	منشف الشعر [سشوار]	monæshshif shaar [sishwār]
iron	مكواة	mækwæ
kettle	غلاية	gællǣyæ
plug	بريزة	prīzæ
radio	راديو	radyo
portable	ترانزيستور	tranzistor
record player	بيك آب	pik-ap
portable	ترانزيستور	tranzistor
shaver	ماكينة حلاقة	mækinit ḥilāka
speakers	مكبرات صوت	mokæbbirǣt sōt

tape recorder	ريكوردر	rikordær
cassette	كاسيت	kasitt
toaster	توستر	tostær
transformer	محول [ترانس]	moḥæwwil [trans]

Record shop

Do you have any records by...	هل عندك اسطوانات لـ ..؟	hæl indæk istiwanāt li
Can I listen to this record?	أريد أن أسمع هذه الاسطوانة من فضلك .	orīd æn æsmæ' hæzihi æl istiwāna min fadlak
I'd like a cassette.	أريد كاسيت .	orīd kasitt
I want a new stylus.	أريد ابرة جديدة .	orīd ibra gædīdæ

33 rpm	٣٣ لفة	tælǣtæ wæ tælætīn læffæ
45 rpm	٤٥ لفة	khæmsæ wæ ærbi'īn læffæ
mono/stereo	مونو / ستريو	mōno/stiryō

Arabic music	موسيقى عربية	mūsīka arabiyyæ
classical music	موسيقى كلاسيك	mūsīka klǣsīk
folk music	موسيقى فولكلورية	mūsīka folklōriyyæ
instrumental music	موسيقى	mūsīka
jazz	موسيقى جاز	mūsīka zhǣz
light music	موسيقى خفيفة	mūsīka khæfīfæ
orchestral music	موسيقى جماعية	mūsīka gæmæ'iyyæ
pop music	موسيقى غربية	mūsīka garbiyya

Here are the names of a few popular recording artists known throughout the Middle East:

Om Kalsoum
Fairouz
Abdel Halim Hafez
Mohamed Abdel Wahab
Farid El Atrash

Warda El Gazaeria
Sabah
Nagat El Saghira
Wadie El Safy
Sabah Fakhri

Hairdressing – At the barber's

I'm in a hurry.	أنا مستعجل .	aenæ mista'gil
I want a haircut, please.	أريد قص الشعر من فضلك .	orīd 'ass il **shaar** min **fad**lak
I'd like a shave.	أريد حلق الذقن .	orīd ḥælk æl zækn
Don't cut it too short.	لا تقصه قصيرا جداً .	læ ta'osso kasiran **gid**dæn
Scissors only, please.	المقص فقط من فضلك .	æl mæ'**ass** fakatt min **fadla**
A razor cut, please.	قص بالموس من فضلك .	'oss bil mūs min **fad**lak
Don't use the clippers.	لا تستعمل الماكينة .	læ tæstææmil æl **mæ**kinæ
Just a trim, please.	قص بسيط من فضلك .	'ass basīt min **fad**lak
That's enough off.	يكفى هذا القص .	**yæk**fi **hæ**zæ æl 'ass
A little more off the...	قصر أكثر من ...	**kassar ak**tar min
back	الخلف	æl khælf
neck	الخلف	æl khælf
sides	الجوانب	æl gæ**wæ**nib
top	أعلى	ææ**l**æ
I don't want any oil.	لا أريد زيت [بريانتين] .	læ **orīd** zēt [briyan**tīn**]
Would you please trim my...?	أريد توضيب ال ... من فضلك .	**orīd** taw**dīb** æl... min **fad**lak
beard	ذقن	zækn
moustache	شنب	**shæ**næbb
sideboards (sideburns)	سوالف	sæ**wæ**lif
Thank you. That's fine.	شكرا . هذا حسن .	shokran. **hæ**zæ **ḥæ**sin
How much do I owe you?	كم الحساب ؟	kæm æl ḥi**sæb**
This is for you.	هذا لك .	**hæ**zæ læk

FOR TIPPING, see inside back cover

Ladies' hairdressing

Is there a hairdresser's in the hotel?	هل يوجد صالون تجميل فى الفندق ؟	hæl **yū**gæd sa**lōn** tægm**īl** fil **fon**dok
Can I make an appointment for sometime on Thursday?	أريد موعداً ليوم الخميس من فضلك .	o**rīd** mæw'id liy**ōm** æl khæ**mīs** min **fad**lak
I'd like it cut and shaped.	أريد قص و تسريح .	o**rīd** 'ass wæ tæs**rīḥ**
with a fringe (bangs)	بفرانجة من الامام	bi **fran**zha minæl 'æm**æ**m
a razor cut	قص بالموس	'ass bil mūs
a re-style	تسريحة جديدة	tæs**rī**ḥæ gæ**dī**dæ
with ringlets	ببوكلات	bi bokl**æ**t
with waves	مموج	mo**mæw**wæg
in a bun	شينيون	shin**yōn**
I want (a)...	أريد ...	o**rīd**
bleach	ازالة اللون	i**zæ**lit æl lōn
colour rinse	غسيل باللون	gæ**sīl** bil lōn
dye	صباغة [تلوين]	si**bā**ga [tæl**wīn**]
permanent	برماننت	pirma**nant**
shampoo and set	شامبو و تسريح	sham**pū** wæ tæs**rīḥ**
tint	لون	lōn
touch up	لمسات	læmæ**sæt**
the same colour	نفس اللون	næfs æl lōn
a darker colour	لون أغمق	lōn æ**g**mak
a lighter colour	لون أفتح	lōn **æf**tæḥ
auburn/blond/ brunette	بنى / أشقر / أسود	**bon**nī/**ash**'ar/**æs**wæd
Do you have a colour chart?	هل عندك دليل للالوان ؟	hæl **in**dæk dæ**līl** lil æl**wæn**
I want a...	أريد ...	o**rīd**
manicure/pedicure	مانيكير / بديكير	mæni**kūr**/pidi**kūr**
face-pack	شد للوجه	shædd lil wægh

FOR DAYS OF THE WEEK, see page 181

Jeweller's—Watchmaker's

Since the days of the pharaohs, handcrafting jewellery has been considered an honoured profession. Moreover, a woman's social status was reflected in the number of jewels she wore. In the markets and jewellery shops of the Middle East, you'll find excellent copies of ancient jewellery—slave bracelets, bangles, snake-shaped bracelets, bedouins' necklaces. Due to cheap local labour, you'll be pleasantly surprised at how inexpensive much jewellery can be. Don't forget, this is the occasion to try your skill at haggling.

Can you repair this watch?	هل يمكنك اصلاح هذه الساعة ؟	hæl yom**kin**æk is**lāḥ** **hǣ**zihi æl **sǣ**æ
The ... is broken.	الـ ... مكسور .	æl... mak**sūr**
glass/spring	زجاج / زمبلك [سوستة]	zo**gǣg**/zæm**bæ**lik [**sos**tæ]
strap/winder	أستيك / مسمار	os**tēk**/mos**mār**
I want this watch cleaned.	أريد تنظيف هذه الساعة .	o**rīd** tan**zīf** **hǣ**zihi æl **sǣ**æ
When will it be ready?	متى تكون جاهزة ؟	mæ**tǣ** tæ**kūn** **gæ**hzæ
Could I please see that?	من فضلك اكشف على هذا .	min **fad**lak **ik**shif **æ**læ **hǣ**zæ
I want a small present for...	أريد هدية صغيرة لـ ...	o**rīd** hæ**diy**yæ sa**gī**ra li
I don't want anything too expensive.	لا أريد شيئاً غالياً .	læ o**rīd** **shæy**'æn **gǣ**liyæn
I want something...	أريد شيئاً . . .	o**rīd** **shæy**'æn
better/cheaper/ simpler	أحسن / أرخص / أبسط	**æḥ**sæn/**ar**khas/**ab**sat
Is this real silver?	هل هذا فضة حقيقية ؟	hæl **hǣ**zæ **fid**da ḥa**kī**kiyya
Have you anything in gold?	هل عندك شيئاً من ذهب ؟	hæl **in**dæk **shæy**'an min **zæ**hæb
How many carats is this?	كم قيراط ؟	kæm ki**rāt**

When you go to a jeweller's, you've probably got some idea of what you want beforehand. Find out what the article is made of and then look up the name for the article itself in the following lists.

What's it made of?

alabaster	الباستر	alabastar
amethyst	رجمشت	rægmæsht
brass	نحاس أصفر	niḥæs asfar
copper	نحاس	niḥæs
coral	مرجان	morgæn
crystal	كريستال	kristæl
cut glass	زجاج مشكل	zogæg moshækkæl
diamond	الماس	almās
ebony	أبنوس	æbænōs
emerald	زمرد	zomorrod
enamel	صدف	sadaf
glass	زجاج	zogæg
gold	ذهب	zæhæb
gold plate	مذهب	mozæhhæb
ivory	عاج	æg
jade	جاد	zhæd
mother-of-pearl	صدف	sadaf
onyx	عقيق	akīk
pearl	لولى	lūli
pewter	معدن	mæædæn
platinum	بلاتين	plætīn
ruby	ياقوت	yæ'ūt
sapphire	ياقوت أزرق	yæ'ūt æzrak
silver	فضة	fidda
silver plate	مفضض	mofaddad
topaz	زبرجد	zæbærgæd
turquoise	فيروز	færūz

What is it?

beads	خرز	**kh**arazz
bracelet	غويشة	giw**ē**shæ
brooch	بروش	brōsh
chain	سلسلة	sil**si**læ
charm	حلية	**ḥil**yæ
cigarette case	علبة سجاير	**il**bit sæ**gǣ**yir
cigarette lighter	ولاعة [قداحة]	wæl**lǣ**æ [æd**dǣ**ḥæ]
clock	ساعة حائط	**sǣ**'it **ḥā**'it
alarm clock	منبه	min**æ**bbih
cross	صليب	sa**līb**
cuff-links	زراير قمصان	zar**ā**yir kom**sān**
cutlery	فضية للاكل	fad**di**yya lil 'ækl
earrings	حلق	**ḥ**ælæk
jewel box	علبة جواهر	**il**bit gæ**wǣ**hir
necklace	عقد	okd
pendant	عليّقة	ol**lē**'æ
pin	دبوس	dæb**būs**
powder compact	علبة بودرة	**il**bit **bo**dra
ring	خاتم	**khǣ**tim
engagement ring	دبلة خطوبة	**dib**lit khot**ū**ba
puzzle ring	خاتم من قطع كثيرة	**khǣ**tim min **ki**taa kæ**sī**ra
signet ring	خاتم رجالى	**khǣ**tim ri**g**æli
wedding ring	دبلة	**dib**læ
rosary	سبحة [مسبحة]	**sib**ḥæ [mæs**b**æḥæ]
silverware	فضية	fad**di**yya
strap	غويشة	gow**ē**shæ
watch strap	أستيك ساعة	os**tēk sǣ**æ
tie-clip	دبوس كرافات	dæb**būs** kra**vāt**
watch	ساعة	**sǣ**æ
pocket watch	ساعة جيب	**sǣ**'it gēb
wrist-watch	ساعة يد	**sǣ**'it yædd

SHOPPING GUIDE

Laundry—Dry cleaning

If your hotel doesn't have its own laundry/dry cleaning service, ask the porter:

Where's the nearest laundry/dry cleaner's?	أين أقرب محل غسيل ومكوة / تنظيف ؟	æynæ akrab mæḥæll gæsīl wæ mækwæ / tanzīf
I want these clothes…	أريد … هذه الملابس .	orid… hæzihi æl mælæbis
cleaned	تنظيف	tanzīf
pressed/ironed	مكوة	mækwit
washed	غسيل	gæsīl
When will it be ready?	متى تكون جاهزة ؟	mætæ tækūn gæhizæ
I need it…	أريدها …	oridohæ
today	اليوم	æl yōm
tomorrow	بكرة	bokra
before Thursday	قبل يوم الخميس	kabl yōm æl khæmīs
Can you … this?	أريد … هذا من فضلك .	orīd… hæzæ min fadlak
mend/patch/stitch	رفة / ترقيع / خياطة	ræffit/tærkī'/khiyātit
Can you sew on this button?	هل يمكنك أن تخيط لى هذا الزر [زرار] ؟	hæl yomkinæk æn tokhayyit lī hæzæ æl zirr [zorār]
Can you get this stain out?	هل يمكنك ازالة هذه البقعة ؟	hæl yomkinæk izælit hæzihi æl bokaa
Can this be invisibly mended?	هل يمكنك رفة هذا دون أن يظهر ؟	hæl yomkinæk ræffit hæzæ dūnæ æn yazhar
This isn't mine.	هذا ليس ملكى .	hæzæ læysæ milki
There's one piece missing.	ناقص قطعة .	nākis kit'a
There's a hole in this.	يوجد ثقب [خرم] فى هذا .	yūgæd sokb [khorm] fi hæzæ
Is my laundry ready?	هل غسيلى جاهز ؟	hæl gæsīli gæhiz

Photography—Cameras

The basic still and home movie exposures are usually given in English in the instructions with the roll.

I want an inexpensive camera.	أريد كاميرا رخيصة .	orīd kæmira rakhīsa

Film

I'd like a...	أريد ...	orīd
cartridge	كارتردج [خزنة الفيلم]	kartridzh [khæznit ilfilm]
film for this camera	فيلم لهذه الكاميرا	film lihæzihi æl kæmira
a ... film	فيلم ...	film
120	١٢٠	miyyæ wæ 'ishrīn
127	١٢٧	miyyæ sæb'æ wæ 'ishrīn
135	١٣٥	miyyæ khæmsæ wæ tælætīn
620	٦٢٠	sottomiyyæ wæ 'ishrīn
8-mm	٨ مم	tæmænyæ milli
super 8	سوبر ٨ مم	sūpar tæmænyæ milli
16-mm	١٦ مم	sittāshar milli
20 exposures	٢٠ صورة	'ishrīn sūra
36 exposures	٣٦ صورة	sittæ wæ tælætīn sūra
this ASA/DIN number	درجة الحساسية ازا / دين	daragit il ḥæsǣsiyyæ aza/din
fast/fine grain	سريع / قليل الحساسية	særiī/kalīl æl hæsǣsiyyæ
black and white	أسود وأبيض	'iswid wabyad
colour	ألوان	'ælwǣn
colour negative	نجاتيف بالالوان	nigætīf bil 'ælwǣn
colour slide	سلايد بالالوان	slayd bil 'ælwǣn
artificial light type	للضوء الصناعى	lil dō' æl sinā'ī
daylight type	لضوء النهار	lidō' æl nahār

FOR NUMBERS, see page 175

Processing

How much do you charge for developing?	بكم التحميض ؟	bikæm æl taḥmīd
I want ... prints of each negative.	أريد ... صورة من كل سلبية [نجاتيف] .	orīd ... sūra min kol sælbiyyæ [nigætīf]

Accessories

I want a/an/some...	أريد ...	orīd
cable release	مفتاح التصوير الآلى	moftæḥ æl taswīr æl'æli
exposure meter	مقياس فتحة العدسة	mikyæs fætḥit æl' ædæsæ
flash bulbs	لمبات الفلاش	lambāt æl flæsh
flash cubes	لمبات فلاش مكعبة	lambāt flæsh mokæ'æbæ
filter	فلتر	filtar
red/yellow	أحمر / أصفر	'aḥmar/'asfar
ultra violet	فوق البنفسجى	fō' æl bænæfsigi
lens cap	غطاء العدسة	gitā' æl 'ædæsæ
lens cleaners	منظف العدسة	monazzif lil 'ædæsæ

Broken

Can you repair this camera?	هل يمكنك اصلاح هذه الكاميرا ؟	hæl yomkinæk 'islāḥ hēzihi æl kæmira
The film is jammed.	الفيلم محشور .	æl film maḥshūr
There's something wrong with the...	الـ ... عطلان .	æl...'atlān
exposure counter	عداد الصور	'æddæd æl sowar
film winder	مفتاح لف الفيلم	moftæḥ læff æl film
lens	عدسة	'ædæsæ
light meter	مقياس الضوء	mikyæs æl dō'
rangefinder	ضابط المسافة	dābit æl mæsæfæ
shutter	منظم فتحة العدسة	monazzim fætḥit æl 'ædæsæ

Provisions

I'd like a/an/some... please.	أريد ... من فضلك .	**orīd**...min **fad**lak
apples	تفاح	toff**ǣḥ**
bananas	موز	mōz
beer	بيرة	**bī**ræ
biscuits (Br.)	بسكويت	bæskæ**wīt**
bread	عيش [خبز]	ēsh [khobz]
butter	زبدة	**zib**dæ
cake	كيك	kēk
candy	حلويات	ḥælæ**wiyyǣt**
cheese	جبنة	**gib**næ
chocolate	شيكولاته	shoko**lā**ta
coffee	قهوة [بن]	**kah**wa [bonn]
cold cuts	لحوم باردة	lo**ḥūm bær**dæ
cookies	بسكويت	bæskæ**wīt**
cooking fat	سمن	**sæm**næ
cream	كريمة	**krē**mæ
eggs	بيض	bēḍ
ice-cream	آيس كريم [جيلاتي]	æys krēm [zhi**lā**ti]
lemonade	لمونادة	læmo**nǣ**tæ
lemons	ليمون [حامض]	læ**mūn** [**ḥā**mid]
lettuce	خس	khass
milk	لبن حليب	**læ**bæn ḥæ**līb**
mustard	مستردة	mos**tar**da
oranges	برتقال	borto**kāl**
pepper	فلفل [بهار]	**fil**fil [bo**hār**]
potatoes	بطاطس	ba**tā**tis
rolls	خبز سندوتش	khobz sændæ**witsh**
salad	صلاطة	sa**lā**ta
salt	ملح	mælḥ
sandwiches	سندوتش	sændæ**witsh**
sausages	سوسيس [سجق/معانق]	sō**sīs** [sogo'/mæ'**ǣ**nik]

sugar	سكر	**sok**kar
sweets	حلويات	hælæwiy**yǣt**
tea	شاى	shǣy
tomatoes	طماطم [بندورة]	ta**mā**tim [bana**dū**ra]
yogurt	زبادى [لبن]	zæ**bǣ**di [**læ**bæn]

And don't forget…

a bottle opener	فتاحة زجاجات	fæt**tǣ**ḥit zo**gǣgǣt**
a corkscrew	فتاحة علب	fæt**tǣ**ḥit **i**læb
matches	كبريت [شحيطة]	kæb**rīt** [shaḥ**ḥā**tæ]
paper napkins	فوط ورق	**fo**watt **wæ**ræk
a tin (can) opener	فتاحة علب	fæt**tǣ**hit **i**læb

Weights and measures

1 kilogram or kilo (kg) = 1000 grams (g)

100 g = 3.5 oz.	½ kg = 1.1 lb.	1 oz. = 28.35 g
200 g = 7.0 oz.	1 kg = 2.2 lb.	1 lb. = 453.60 g

1 litre (l) = 0.88 imp. quarts = 1.06 U.S. quarts

1 imp. quart = 1.14 l	1 U.S. quart = 0.95 l
1 imp. gallon = 4.55 l	1 U.S. gallon = 3.8 l

box	علبة	**il**bæ
carton	صندوق كارتون	son**dūk** kar**tōn**
jar	أبريق	æb**rī'**
packet	باكو	**bǣ**ko
tin (can)	علبة صفيح	**il**bæ sa**fīḥ**
tube	أنبوبة	on**bū**bæ
gram	جرام	grām
pound	رطل	ratl
kilogram	كيلوجرام	kilo**grām**
litre	لتر	litr

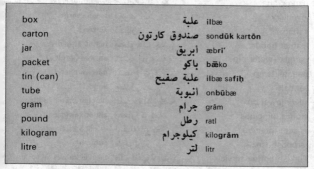

Souvenirs

Browsing through the bustling markets will turn up countless treasured souvenirs of your visit to the Middle East. Jewellery and precious stones will certainly interest the ladies. Ceramics, glassware, sandals and hand-embroidered garments also make especially appreciated gifts.

Below are a few suggestions for souvenirs you might like to bring home:

antiques	انتيكات	ænti**kǣt**
backgammon set	طاولة زهر	**taw**lit zahr
brass and copper objects	مصنوعات نحاس	masnū**'āt** ni**ḥǣs**
carpets	سجاجيد	sægǣ**gid**
ceramics	فخار	fokh**khār**
cutlery (Lebanon)	فضية	fad**diy**ya
dagger	خنجر	**khan**gar
glass (hand-blown)	زجاج	**zogǣg**
gold filigree	ذهب مشغول	**d**æhæb mæsh**gūl**
hand-embroidered garments	ملابس تطريز يدوى	mæ**lǣ**bis tat**rīz yæ**dæwi
handicrafts	صناعات يدوية	sina**āt** gil**diy**yæ
jewellery	مجوهرات	mogawha**rāt**
kaftan	قفطان	kof**tān**
leather goods	مصنوعات جلدية	masnū**'āt** gil**diy**yæ
nargile (water pipe)	شيشة [أرجيلة]	**shī**shæ [ær**gī**læ]
oriental lamp	مصباح شرقى	mis**bāḥ shar**ki
sandals	صندل	**san**dal
silver jewel box	علبة جواهر فضة	**il**bit gæ**wǣ**hir **fad**da
stones, precious	أحجار كريمة	aḥ**gār** kæ**rī**mæ
semi-precious	شبه كريمة	shibh kæ**rī**mæ
tarboosh (fez)	طربوش	tar**būsh**
Turkish coffee service	طقم للقهوة التركى	takm lil **kah**wa æl **tor**ki

Tobacconist's

You'll find the typical oriental cigarettes (e.g., *Cleopatra* in Egypt, *Bafra* or *Khanon* in Lebanon) lighter than those at home. The reason is that the young tobacco leaves are harvested before they mature. Brands that are manufactured locally are quite cheap. Foreign cigarettes are considerably more expensive.

Give me a/an some..., please.	أريد ... من فضلك .	**orīd**... min **fad**lak
cigars	سيجار	sīgār
cigarette case	علبة لحمل السجاير	**'il**bæ liḥæml æl sæ**gǣ**yir
cigarette holder	فم سجاير	fomm sæ**gǣ**yir
flints	حجر ولاعة [قداحة]	**ḥa**gar wæl**lǣ**æ ['æd**dǣ**ḥæ]
lighter	ولاعة [قداحة]	wæl**lǣ**æ ['æd**dǣ**ḥæ]
lighter fluid/gas	بنزين / غاز ولاعة [قداحة]	bæn**zīn**/gǣz wæl**lǣ**æ ['æd**dǣ**ḥæ]
matches	كبريت [شحيطة]	kæb**rīt** [shaḥ**ḥē**ta]
packet of cigarettes	علبة سجاير	**'il**bit sæ**gǣ**yir
packet of *Cleopatras*	علبة كليوباترة	**'il**bit kilyō**ba**tra
pipe	بايب	payp
pipe tobacco	دخان بايب	dokh**kaǣn** payp
pipe cleaners	منظف بايب	mo**naz**zif payp
tobacco pouch	باكو دخان بايب	**bǣ**ko dokh**khǣn** payp
Have you any...?	عندك ... ؟	**æn**dæk
American cigarettes	سجاير أمريكانى	sæ**gǣ**yir 'æmri**kǣ**ni
English cigarettes	سجاير انجليزى	sæ**gǣ**yir 'ingi**lī**zi
menthol cigarettes	سجاير منتول	sæ**gǣ**yir min**tol**
I'd like a carton.	أريد خرطوشة .	**orīd** khar**tū**sha

filter-tipped	بفم فلتر	bi**fomm fil**tær
without filter	بدون فلتر	bi**dūn fil**tær

TOBACCONIST'S

Your money: banks—currency

In the Middle East, there's generally no import limit on foreign currency. In Egypt, on the other hand, no Egyptian currency may be brought in or taken out of the country, and all foreign currency brought in must be declared. When you change money, don't forget to ask for a receipt or have the transaction noted on your D (declaration) form. When leaving Egypt, customs will ask you either for your receipts or your D form.

Monetary unit

Egypt: 1 Egyptian pound (£E) = 100 piastres (pts.) = 1,000 mil.

Jordan: 1 Jordanian dinar (JD) = 1,000 fils (fls.)

Lebanon: 1 Lebanese pound (£L) = 100 piastres (pts.)

	Bank-notes	Coins
Egypt	5, 10, 25, 50 pts. 1, 5, 10£E	½, 1, 5, 10 pts.
Jordan	500 fls.; 1, 5, 10, 50 JD	1, 5, 10, 20, 50, 100 fls.
Lebanon	1, 5, 10, 25, 50, 100 L£	1, 2½, 5, 10, 25, 50 pts.

Banking hours

Egypt: 8.30 a.m. – 12.30 p.m., daily except Friday; Sunday 10 a.m. to noon.

Jordan: 8.30 a.m. – 1 p.m. and 3.30 p.m. – 7.30 p.m.; Saturday to Thursday.

Lebanon: 8.30 a.m. – 12.30 p.m., Monday to Friday; Saturday 8.30 a.m. – 12 a.m.

Before going

Where's the nearest...? bank/currency exchange?	أين أقرب بنك / مكتب كامبيو ؟	æynæ 'akrab bænk/ mæktæb kæmbyo
Where can I cash a traveller's cheque (check)?	أين يمكن صرف شيكات سياحية ؟	æynæ yomkin sarf shēkæt siyæḥiyyæ
Where's the American Express?	أين الأميريكان اكسبريس؟	æynæ æl 'æmirikæn iksprēs

Inside

I want to change some dollars/pounds.	أريد تحويل دولارات / جنيهات استرلينى .	orīd tæḥwīl dolārāt/ gonæyhæt 'istirlīni
What's the exchange rate?	ما سعر التحويل ؟	mæ siir æl tæḥwīl
What rate of commission do you charge?	ما العمولة التى يأخذها البنك ؟	mæ æl 'omulæ ællæti yæ'khozohæ æl bænk
Can you cash a personal cheque?	هل تصرف شيكات خاصة ؟	hæl tasrif shēkæt khāssa
How long will it take to clear?	ما طول مدة المراجعة ؟	mæ tūl moddit æl moræg'æ
Can you wire my bank in London?	هل يمكنك أن ترسل تلغراف الى بنكى فى لندن ؟	hæl yomkinæk æn torsil tælligrāf 'ilæ bænki fi landan
I have...	عندى ...	'indi
a letter of credit	خطاب ضمان	khitāb damān
an introduction from...	خطاب من ...	khitāb min
a credit card	بطاقة رصيد مصرفى	bitākit rasīd masrafi
I'm expecting some money from... Has it arrived yet?	أنا منتظر فلوس من ... هل وصلت ؟	ænæ montazir folūs min... hæl wasalæt
Please give me... 10-pound notes (bills) and some small change.	من فضلك اعطنى ... ورقة من فئة العشرة جنيهات وبعض الفكـّـة [الفراطة]	min fadlak aatini...waraka min fi'æt 10 gonæyhæt wa baad æl fækkæ [æl frāta]

Give me... large notes and the rest in small notes.	اعطنى ... ورقة من فئة كبيرة والباقى فئاَت صغيرة.	aatinī... **wa**raka min **fi**'æ kæ**bī**ræ wæl **bā**ki fi'**ǣt** saġīra
Could you please check that again?	من فضلك راجع هذا .	min **fad**lak **rǣ**gii **hǣ**zæ
I want to credit this to my account.	أريد ايداع هذا فى حسابى .	**orīd** 'i**dǣ**æ **hǣ**zæ fī ḥi**sǣ**bī
Where should I sign?	أين أوقع ؟	æynæ o**wakki**'

Currency converter

In a world of fluctuating currencies, we can offer no more than this do-it-yourself chart. You can get a card showing current exchange rates from banks, travel agents and tourist offices. Why not fill in this chart, too, for handy reference?

	£	$
10 Egyptian piastres		
50		
1 Egyptian pound		
5		
10		
100 Jordanian fils		
500		
1 Jordanian dinar		
5		
10		
1 Lebanese pound		
5		
10		
50		
100		

At the post office

In Egypt post offices are open from 8.30 a.m. to 3 p.m. except Sundays when they open only in the morning. They remain closed all day Friday. Big hotels usually have all post office facilities at the reception.

In Jordan the post offices are open from 8 a.m. to 2 p.m. except Friday when they are closed all day.

In Lebanon, mail, telex and telegram service is available from 8.30 a.m. to 1 p.m. except Friday. At least in Beirut, you can telephone from the post office 24 hours a day.

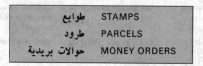

Where's the nearest post office?	أين أقرب مكتب بريد ؟	æynæ **akrab mæk**tæb bæ**rīd**
What time does the post office open/close?	متى يفتح / يقفل مكتب البريد ؟	mætæ **yæf**tæḥ/**yak**fil **mæk**tæb æl bæ**rīd**
What window do I go to for stamps?	أين شباك الطوابع ؟	æynæ shib**bæk** æl ta**wā**bii
At which counter can I cash an international money order?	فى أى شباك يمكننى صرف حوالة بريدية أجنبية ؟	min æyy shib**bæk** yom**ki**noni sarf ho**wæ**læ bæ**ri**diyyæ ægnæ**bi**yyæ
I want some stamps, please.	أريد طوابع من فضلك .	orīd tawābi' min **fad**lak
What's the postage for a letter to England?	بكم الخطاب لانجلترا ؟	bi**kæm** ælkhi**tāb** li 'ingil**ti**ra
What's the postage for a postcard to the U.S.A.?	ما الثمن لارسال كارت بوستال الى أمريكا ؟	mæ ælt**æ**mæn li 'ir**sæl** kært pos**tæl** 'ilæ 'æm**rī**kæ

طوابع	STAMPS
طرود	PARCELS
حوالات بريدية	MONEY ORDERS

Do all letters go airmail?	هل كـل الخطابات تسافر بالبريد الجوى ؟	hæl koll æl khitā**bāt** tosǣfir bil bæ**rīd** æl **gæ**wwi
I want to send this parcel.	أريد ارسال هذا الطرد .	o**rīd** 'ir**sǣl** **hǣ**zæl tard
Do I need to fill in a customs declaration?	هل يجب أن أملأ استمارة الجمرك ؟	hæl **yæ**gib æn **'æ**mlæ' 'istimā**rit** æl **gom**rok
Where's the mailbox?	أين صندوق الخطابات ؟	æynæ son**dūk** æl khitā**bāt**
I want to send this by...	أريد ارسال هذا ...	o**rīd** 'ir**sǣl** **hǣ**zæ
airmail	بالبريد الجوى	bil bæ**rīd** æl **gæ**wwi
express (special delivery)	بالبريد المستعجل	bil bæ**rīd** æl mostæ**æ**gæl
registered mail	بالبريد المسجل	bil bæ**rīd** æl mo**sæg**gæl
Where's the poste restante (general delivery)?	أين مكتب تسليم الخطابات ؟	æynæ **mæk**tæb tæs**līm** æl khitā**bāt**
Is there any mail for me? My name is...	هل توجد خطابات لى ؟ اسمى ...	hæl **tū**gæd kitā**bāt** li? **'is**mi
Here's my passport.	هذا باسبورى .	**hǣ**zæ pas**pō**ri

Telegrams

I want to send a telegram. May I please have a form?	أريد ارسال تلغراف . من فضلك اعطنى استمارة .	o**rīd** 'ir**sǣl** tælli**grāf**. min **fad**lak aatini 'istimā**ra**
How much is it per word?	بكم الكلمة ؟	bi**kæm** æl **kil**mæ
How long will a cable to Boston take?	متى يصل التلغراف الى بوسطون ؟	**mæ**tǣ yasil æl tælli**grāf** **'i**lǣ **bos**ton
I'd like to reverse the charges.	أريد أن يدفع المستلم ثمن التلغراف .	o**rīd** 'æn **yæd**fææ æl mostælim **tæ**mæn æl tælli**grāf**
I'd like to send a letter-telegram (night-letter).	أريد ارسال تلغراف .L.T .	o**rīd** 'ir**sǣl** tælli**grāf** æl ti

Telephoning

You won't find any telephone booths in Egypt and Jordan except at the post office. When you want to make a local call, you can go into a store. If you want to call long distance, you'll have to go to a post office or a big hotel.

In Lebanon calls can be made from telephone booths or from restaurants, cafés or hotels. Public telephones are coin operated: insert the appropriate coins and then dial. When the other person answers, push the white button to complete the connection.

Where's the telephone?	أين التليفون ؟	æynæl tili**fōn**
May I use your phone?	هل يمكنني استعمال التليفون ؟	hæl yom**ki**noni 'istii**mǣl** æl tili**fōn**
Do you have a telephone directory of Beirut?	هل عندك دليل تليفونات بيروت ؟	hæl '**in**dæk dæ**līl** tilifō**nǣt** bæy**rūt**
Can you help me get this number?	من فضلك ساعدني في الاتصال بهذا الرقم .	min **fad**lak sǣ'**id**ni fil 'itti**sāl** bi**hǣ**zæ æl **ra**kam

Operator

Do you speak English?	هل تتكلم انجليزى ؟	hæl tætæ**kæl**læm ingi**līzi**
Good morning, I want Cairo 123456.	صباح الخير . أريد القاهرة ١٢٣٤٥٦ .	sa**bāḥ** æl khēr. o**rīd** ælkāhira 123 456
Can I dial direct?	هل يوجد خط مباشر ؟	hæl **yū**gæd khatt mo**bǣ**shir
I want to place a personal (person-to-person) call.	أريد مكالمة شخصية .	o**rīd** mo**kæl**mæ shakh**siy**yæ
I want to reverse the charges.	أريد أن يدفع الشخص المطلوب ثمن المكالمة .	o**rīd** æn **yæd**fææ æl shakhs æl mat**lūb** **tæ**mæn æl mo**kæl**mæ
Will you tell me the cost of the call afterwards?	هل يمكنك أن تخبرني بثمن المكالمة فيما بعد ؟	hæl yom**ki**næk æn tokh**bir**ni bitæmæn æl mo**kæl**mæ **fī**mæ **bæ**æd

Speaking

Hello. This is... speaking.	آلو . أنا ..	**ælō. 'ænæ**
I want to speak to...	أريد أن أتحدث الى ...	**orīd** æn 'ætæ**ḥæd**dæs 'ilæ
Would you put me through to...?	من فضلك اعطنى ... ؟	min **fad**lak aatini
I want extension...	أريد الداخلى رقم ...	**orīd** æl dæ**khi**li **ra**kam
Is that...?	هل هذا ... ؟	hæl **hæ**zæ

Bad luck

Would you please try again later?	من فضلك حاول مرة أخرى فيما بعد .	min **fad**lak **ḥæ**wil **mar**ra '**okh**ra **fī**mæ **bæ**æd
Operator, you gave me the wrong number.	لقد أعطيتنى نمرة غلط .	la**kad** aataytæni **nim**ræ **ga**lat
Operator, we were cut off.	انقطعت المكالمة .	'in**ka**ta'æt æl mo**kæl**mæ

Not there

When will he/she be back?	متى يرجع / ترجع ؟	**mæ**tæ **yær**gaa/**tær**gaa
Will you tell him/her I called?	من فضلك قل له / لها انى اتصلت .	min **fad**lak kol **læ**ho/**læ**hæ **in**ni itta**salt**
My name's...	اسمى ...	**is**mi
Would you ask him/her to call me?	من فضلك اطلب منه / منها الاتصال بى .	min **fad**lak **ot**lob **min**ho/**min**hæ æl 'itti**sāl** bī
Would you please take a message?	من فضلك خذ هذه الرسالة .	min **fad**lak khozz **hæ**zihi æl ri**sæ**læ

Charges

What was the cost of that call?	بكم هذه المكالمة ؟	**bikæm hæzihi** æl **mokælmæ**
I want to pay for the call.	أريد أن أدفع ثمن المكالمة .	**orid** 'æn '**æd**fææ **tæ**mæn æl **mokælmæ**

توجد مكالمة تليفونية لك .	There's a telephone call for you.
ما النمرة التى تطلبها ؟	What number are you calling?
الخط مشغول .	The line's engaged.
لا يرد أحد .	There's no answer.
النمرة غلط .	You've got the wrong number.
التليفون عطلان .	The phone is out of order.
هو خرج / هى خرجت .	He's/She's out at the moment.

FOR SPELLING, see page 11

The car

Filling station

We'll start this section by considering your possible needs at a filling station.

Where's the nearest filling station?	أين أقرب محطة بنزين ؟	æynæ **ak**rab ma**ḥat**tit bæn**zīn**
I want...litres of petrol (gas), please.	أريد ... لتر بنزين من فضلك .	o**rīd**...litr bæn**zīn** min **fad**lak
ten/twenty/fifty	عشرة / عشرين / خمسين	'ashara/'ish**rīn**/khæm**sīn**
I want...litres of standard/premium.	أريد ... لتر بنزين عادى / سوبر .	o**rīd**...litr bæn**zīn** '**ǣ**dī/ **sū**par
Fill the tank, please.	املأها من فضلك .	im**lǣ**hǣ min **fad**lak
Please check the oil and water.	من فضلك اكشف على الزيت والماء .	min **fad**lak **ik**shif ælǣ æl zēt wæl mǣ'
Give me...litres of oil.	اعطنى ... لتر زيت .	'ā**tī**ni...litr zēt
Fill up the battery with distilled water.	املأ البطارية بماء مقطّر .	**im**læ' æl bat**tā**riyya bi**ma**yya mokat**ta**ra
Check the brake fluid.	اكشف على زيت الفرامل .	**ik**shif ælǣ zēt æl fa**rā**mil

Fluid measures

litres	imp. gal.	U.S. gal.	litres	imp. gal.	U.S. gal.
5	1.1	1.3	30	6.6	7.9
10	2.2	2.6	35	7.7	9.2
15	3.3	4.0	40	8.8	10.6
20	4.4	5.3	45	9.9	11.9
25	5.5	6.6	50	11.0	13.2

FOR NUMBERS, see page 175

Would you check the tires?	من فضلك اكشف على ضغط العجل [الدواليب] .	min **fad**lak **'ik**shif 'ælǣ dagt æl **'æ**gæl [æl dwælīb]
The pressure should be 23 front, 26 rear.	الضغط ٢٣ للأمام و ٢٦ للخلف .	æl dagt 23 lil 'æ**mǣm** wæ 26 lil khælf
Check the spare tire, too, please.	من فضلك اكشف على الاستبن .	min **fad**lak **'ik**shif 'ælæl 'is**tibn**
Can you mend this puncture (fix this flat)?	من فضلك اصلح هذه العجلة [الدولاب] .	min **fad**lak **'as**liḥ hǣzihi æl 'ægælæ [æl dū**lǣb**]
Will you change this tire, please?	من فضلك غيّر هذه العجلة [الدولاب] .	min **fad**lak **gæy**yir hǣ**zi**hi æl 'ægælæ [æl dū**lǣb**]
Will you clean the windshield (windscreen)?	من فضلك نظف الزجاج الأمامى .	min **fad**lak **naz**zif æl zo**gǣg** æl 'æ**mǣ**mi
Have you a road map of this area?	هل عندك خريطة للطرق فى هذه المنطقة .	hæl **'in**dæk kharīta lil **to**rok fi hǣ**zi**hi æl man**tika**
Where are the toilets?	أين التواليت ؟	æynæl twæ**lit**

Asking the way—Street directions

Excuse me.	من فضلك !	min **fad**lak
Can you tell me the way to...?	ما هو الطريق الى ... ؟	mǣ **ho**wæ æl ta**rīk** 'ilǣ
How do I get to...?	كيف أصل الى ... ؟	**kæy**fæ **'a**sil 'ilǣ
Where does this road lead to?	الى أين يؤدى هذا الطريق ؟	'ilæ 'æynæ yo'**æd**dī **hǣ**zæ æl ta**rīk**
Can you show me on this map where I am?	من فضلك اشر لى على مكانى على الخريطة .	min **fad**lak 'æshir li 'ælǣ mæ**kǣ**ni 'ælæl kharīta
How far is it to... from here?	ما هى المسافة الى ...	mǣ **hi**yæ æl mæs**ǣ**fæ 'ilǣ

CAR—SERVICE STATION

Miles into kilometres

1 mile = 1.609 kilometres (km)

miles	10	20	30	40	50	60	70	80	90	100
km	16	32	48	64	80	97	113	129	145	161

Kilometres into miles

1 kilometre (km) = 0.62 miles

km	10	20	30	40	50	60	70	80	90	100	110	120	130
miles	6	12	19	25	31	37	44	50	56	62	68	75	81

انك على طريق غلط .	You're on the wrong road.
أذهب الى الأمام .	Go straight ahead.
انه هناك على الشمال (اليمين) .	It's down there on the left (right).
اذهب من هذا الطريق ...	Go that way.
اذهب الى أول (ثانى) تقاطع .	Go to the first (second) crossroads.
انحن الى الشمال (اليمين) عند الاشارة .	Turn left (right) at the traffic lights.

In the rest of this section we'll be more closely concerned with the car itself. We've divided it into two parts:

Part A contains general advice on motoring in the Middle East. It's essentially for reference and is therefore to be browsed over, preferably in advance.

Part B is concerned with the practical details of accidents and breakdown. It includes a list of car parts and a list of things that may go wrong with them. Just show it to the garage mechanic and have him point to the items required.

Part A

Customs—Documentation

Visitors will require the following documents to get their car through customs:

Passport and visa
International driving licence
Car registration papers (log book)*
Tryptic (customs pass booklet for vehicle); not required in Lebanon if you are travelling on a tourist visa

Insurance requirements vary from country to country:

Egypt requires that tourists obtain insurance in order to drive in the country. The International Motor Insurance Certificate (Green Card) is recognized only if Egypt is specifically mentioned on the document. If you haven't taken out an insurance extension before leaving home, you can get coverage at your arrival point in Egypt or through the Egyptian Touring Club Association.

Lebanon has no compulsory insurance requirements, but the Green Card is recognized provided Lebanon is specifically mentioned on the document. Insurance can also be obtained upon arrival through an insurance company in Beirut.

Jordan has no compulsory insurance requirements. It would be advisable, before leaving home, to have your regular insurance policy extended to cover travel in the Middle East. However, coverage can also be obtained locally if needed be.

Though the above information is up to date as we go to press, it is advisable to check with your automobile association or the appropriate consulate before you leave home.

* Egypt requires an international car registration document, obtainable through your local automobile association.

Here's my...	هذا / هذه ...	hǣzæ/hǣzihi
driving licence	رخصة القيادة	rokhsit ælkiyǣdæ
insurance policy	بوليصة التأمين	bolīsit æltæ'mīn
green card	بوليصة التأمين الدولية	bolīsit æltæ'mīn ældæwliyyæ
passport	باسبورى	paspōri
I haven't anything to declare.	ليس عندى أى شيء أعلن عنه .	læysæ 'indi 'æyy shē' 'oolin 'ænho
I've...	عندى ...	'indi
a carton of cigarettes	خرطوشة سجاير	khartūshit sægǣyir
a bottle of whisky	زجاجة وسكى	zogǣgit wiski
a bottle of wine	زجاجة نبيت	zogǣgit nibīt
We're staying for...	سنبقى ...	sænabkā
a week	أسبوع	'osbū'
2 weeks*	أسبوعين	'osbūēn
a month	شهر	shahr

Roads

Roads—especially main highways—in the Arab countries are generally good and road signs are usually given in English. We recommend prudent driving until you're familiar with the roads, signs and the driving habits of the local drivers. You'll find that drivers make extensive use of their horns. Don't let this scare you; just be sure to follow the traffic rules.

Pedestrian crossings are marked by white zebra stripes, but the security they seem to offer is often illusory.

Distances are marked in kilometres, and the main highways have road signs. There are rest areas *(isteraha)* at frequent intervals where you can refuel, check your car or make minor repairs while having a drink or snack.

* see grammar

Arab highways are not fenced, and night driving at high speed is dangerous, particularly on desert roads between Alexandria and Cairo where you may unconsciously stray into the desert unless you are alert to the road verge markings.

Speed limits in Arabic countries are as follows:

	Residential areas	Open highways
cars	50 km/h (30 mph)	90 km/h (56 mph)
motorcycles	40 km/h (25 mph)	70 km/h (44 mph)

Parking

Use your common sense when parking. The police are normally reasonably lenient with tourists, but don't push your luck too far. You can be fined on the spot for traffic offenses.

In Egypt, in addition to parking meters, you'll find car parks, where a versatile attendant will park your car for you, if necessary by moving other cars to create a space. He may ask you to leave your handbrake off to facilitate his work of shuffling cars around. You'll recognize him by his special badge. It's customary to give the attendant a small tip for his services.

Excuse me. May I park here?	ممكن أركن [أصف] هنا من فضلك ؟	**mom**kin 'ærkin ['a**siff**] **ho**næ min **fad**lak
How long may I park here?	ما مدة الركن [الصف] المسموحة ؟	mæ **mod**dit æl rækn [æl saff] æl mæs**mūḥ**æ
What's the charge for parking here?	بكم الركن [الصف] هنا ؟	**bikæm** æl rækn [æl saff] **honæ**
Must I leave my lights on?	هل يجب أن أترك النور ؟	hæl yæ**gib** 'æn '**æt**rok æl nūr

Road signs

You'll find that many of the standard international road signs are used in the Arab countries. Some special ones are shown on pages 160–161.

Here are some of the main written signs you're likely to encounter when driving in the Middle East.

الطريق يضيق	Road narrows
احترس	Caution
احترس ، أطفال	Attention, children
الزم اليمين	Keep right
تحويلة	Diversion (Detour)
خطر	Danger
طريق منزلق	Slippery road
طريق سريع	Motorway (Expressway)
عبور مشاة	Pedestrians
مزلقان	Level-crossing (Railroad crossing)
قف	Stop
ممنوع الانتظار	No parking
ممنوع الدخول	No entry
مستشفى	Hospital
منحنى خطر	Dangerous bend (curve)
ممنوع تخطى السيارة التى أمامك	No overtaking (No passing)
موقف سيارات	Parking
مدرسة	School
منطقة عمل	Road works (Men working)
هدوء	Silence
شارع اتجاه واحد	One-way street
هدئ السرعة	Slow
هدئ السرعة	Drive slowly

FOR ROAD SIGNS, see also pages 160–161

Part B

Accidents

This section is confined to immediate aid. The legal problems of responsibility and settlement can be taken care of at a later stage. Your first concern will be for the injured.

Is anyone hurt?	هل أصيب أحد ؟	hæl os**i**bæ ʼæḥæd
Don't move.	لا تتحرك .	lǣ tætæ**ḥ**arrak
It's all right. Don't worry.	لا تقلق . كل شىء على ما يرام .	læ **tæ**ʼlæʼ. kol shēʼ ʼælǣ mǣ yor**ā**m
Where's the nearest telephone?	أين أقرب تليفون ؟	æynæ ʼ**a**krab tili**fō**n
Can I use your telephone? There's been an accident.	هل يمكننى استعمال تليفونك ؟ فيه حادثه .	hæl yom**k**inoni ʼistii**mǣl** tili**fō**næk? fih **ḥæ**dsæ
Call a doctor/ ambulance quickly.	اطلب دكتور / سيارة اسعاف بسرعة .	**ot**lob dok**tō**r/sæy**yā**rit ʼisæ**ǣf** bis**o**raa
There are people injured.	هناك مصابون .	hon**ǣk** mos**ā**b**ū**n
Help me get them out of the car.	ساعدنى على اخراجهم من السيارة .	sǣʼ**id**ni ʼælǣ ʼikhr**ā**gihim min æl sæy**yā**ra

Police—Exchange of information

Please call the police.	من فضلك اطلب البوليس .	min **fad**lak **ʼot**lob æl bo**lī**s
There's been an accident. It's about 3 kilometres from...	لقد وقع حادث على بعد ٣ كيلومتر من ...	la**kad wa**kaa **ḥǣ**dis ʼælǣ **bood** 3 kilo**mitr** min
I'm on the Cairo–Alexandria road, 25 kilometres from Alexandria.	أنا على طريق مصر – اسكندرية على بعد ٢٥ كيلومتر من الاسكندرية .	ʼæ**nǣ** ælǣ ta**rīk** masr–ʼiskindi**riy**yæ ʼælǣ **bood** 25 kilo**mitr** minæl ʼiskændæ**riy**yæ
Here's my name and address.	هذا اسمى وعنوانى .	**hǣ**zæ ʼ**is**mi wæ ʼin**nǣ**ni

Would you mind acting as a witness?	هل يمكنك أن تشهد ؟	hæl yomkinæk 'æn tæshhæd
I'd like an interpreter.	أريد مترجم .	orīd motærgim

Remember to put out a red triangle warning if the car is out of action or impeding traffic.

Breakdown

...and that's what we'll do with this section: break it down into four phases.

1. *On the road*
   You ask where the nearest garage is.
2. *At the garage*
   You tell the mechanic what's wrong.
3. *Finding the trouble*
   He tells you what he thinks is wrong.
4. *Getting it fixed*
   You tell him to fix it and, once that's done, settle the account (or argue about it).

Phase 1—On the road

Where's the nearest garage?	أين أقرب جراج ؟	æynæ 'akrab garāzh
Excuse me. My car has broken down. May I use your phone?	سيارتى تعطلت . هل يمكننى استخدام تليفونك من فضلك ؟	sæyyārati ta'attalat. hæl yomkinoni 'istikhdǣm tilifōnæk min fadlak
What's the telephone number of the nearest garage?	ما نمرة تليفون أقرب جراج ؟	mǣ nimrit tilifōn akrab garāzh
I've had a breakdown at...	تعطلت سيارتى عند ...	ta'attalat sæyyārati 'indæ

We are on the Beirut–Tripoli road, about 10 kilometres from Beirut.	نحن على طريق بيروت – طرابلس ، على بعد ١٠ كم من بيروت .	næḥno ælǣ tarīk bæy-rūt–tarablos ælǣ bood ashara kilomitr min bæyrūt
Can you send a mechanic?	من فضلك ارسل لنا ميكانيكى .	min fadlak arsil lænǣ mikænīki
Can you send a truck to tow my car?	من فضلك ارسل لنا لورى لسحب السيارة .	min fadlak arsil lænǣ lōri lisæḥb ælsayyāra
How long will you be?	متى ترجع ؟	mætǣ targaa

Phase 2—At the garage

Can you help me?	هل يمكنك مساعدتى ؟	hæl yomkinæk mosǣ'æ-dæti
I don't know what's wrong with it.	لا أعرف ما بها .	lǣ aaraf mǣ bihǣ
I think there's something wrong with the...	أظن أن ... به عيب .	azonn ænnæ...bihi ēb
axle	محور العجلة	miḥwar æl 'ægælæ
battery	البطارية	æl battariyya
brakes	الفرامل	æl farāmil
clutch	الدبرياج	æl dibriyǣzh
contact	الكونتاكت	æl kontækt
dip (dimmer) switch	مفتاح النور	moftǣḥ æl nūr
direction indicator	الاشارة	æl 'ishāra
door	البـاب	æl bǣb
dynamo	الدينامو	æl dinamō
electrical system	الكهرباء	æl kahraba
engine	الموتور	æl motōr
fuel feed	خرطوم البنزين	khartūm æl bænzīn
gears	التروس	æl torūs
generator	الدينامو	æl dinæmō
horn	آلة التنبيه [الكلاكسون]	'ǣlæt æl tænbīh [klækson]
ignition system	المـارش	æl marsh

CAR—REPAIRS

lights	النور	æl 'adwā'
brake lights	نور الفرامل	nūr æl farāmil
headlights	النور الأمامى	æl nūr æl 'æmææmi
rear (tail) lights	النور الخلفى	æl nūr æl khælfi
reversing (backup) lights	نور السير للخلف	nūr æl marsh khælfi
muffler	ماسورة العادم [الشكمان]	masūrit æl ādim [æl shækmææn]
oil system	الزيت	æl zēt
radiator	الرادياتير	æl radiatēr
seat	الكرسى	æl korsi
silencer	ماسورة العادم [الشكمان]	masūrit æl ādim [æl shækmææn]
speedometer	عداد السرعة	æddææd æl soraa
starter motor	الاستارتر [المارش]	æl 'istartir [æl marsh]
steering	عجلة القيادة [الدركسيون]	ægælit æl kiyādæ [æl diriksyōn]
suspension	السوست [السسبنسيون]	æl sosæt [æl sospænsyōn]
transmission	عمود الكردان	æmūd ælkirdææn
turn signal	الاشارة	æl 'ishāra
wheels	العجل [الدواليب]	æl ægæl [æl dwalīb]
wipers	المساحات	æl mæssæḥææt

LEFT	RIGHT
يسار	يمين
(yæsār)	(yæmīn)

FRONT	BACK
أمـام	خلف
('æmææm)	(khælf)

It's (too) ...	انه ...	innæho
backfiring	يصفق	yosaffik
bad	سيىء	sæyyi'
blown	ضارب	dārib
broken	مكسور	maksūr
burnt	محترق	moḥtarik
chafing	يحتك	yæḥtækk
cracked	مشقوق	mæshkūk

defective	بـايظ	bāyiz
disconnected	غير واصل	gēr wāsil
dry	جـاف	gæff
jammed	مزنوق	mæznū'
jerking	يخبط	yokhabbitt
knocking	يدق	yædok
leaking	يخر	yækhorr
loose	مفكوك	mæfkūk
noisy	يسبب صوتاً	yosæbbib sawtan
overheating	يسبب سخونة شديدة	yosæbbib sokhūnæ shædīdæ
slack	غير مشدود	gēr mæshdūd
slipping	ينزلق [يزحط]	yænzalik [yozaḥḥit]
split	منقسم	monkasim
stuck	مزنوق	mæznū'
vibrating	يهتز	yæhtæzz
weak	ضعيف	da'īf
The car won't start.	السيارة لا تدور .	æl sayyāra lǣ tadūr
The car won't pull.	السيارة لا تسحب .	æl sayyāra lǣ tæsḥæb
The car is making a funny noise.	السيارة بها صوت غريب .	æl sayyāra bihǣ sōt gærīb
It's locked and the keys are inside.	السيارة مقفولة والمفتاح بداخلها .	æl sayyāra mæskūkæ wæl moftǣḥ bidǣkhilhǣ
The radiator is leaking.	الرادياتير يخر .	æl radyatēr yækhorr
The clutch engages too quickly.	الدبرياج يفلت بسرعة .	æl dibriyǣzh yæflit bisoraa
The steering wheel's vibrating.	عجلة القيادة تهتز .	'ægælit æl kiyāda tæhtæzz
The suspension is weak.	السوست [السسبنسيون] ضعيفة .	æl sosætt [æl sospænsyōn] da'īfa
The...needs adjusting.	الـ ... محتاج الى ضبط .	æl... moḥtǣg ilǣ dabt
brake/clutch/idling	فرامل/دبرياج/سيلانسيه	farāmil/dibriyǣzh/silansyēh

Now that you've explained what's wrong, you'll want to know how long it will take to repair it and arrange yourself accordingly.

How long will it take to repair?	ما مدة التصليح ؟	mæ tūl **moddæt** æl tas**līḥ**
Suppose I come back tomorrow?	هل أرجع بكرة ؟	hæl **argaa bokra**
Can you give me a lift into town?	هل يمكنك توصيلى الى المدينة ؟	hæl yom**kinæk** taw**sīli** ilæ ælmæ**dīnæ**
Is there a place to stay nearby?	هل يوجد مكان قريب للبقاء فيه ؟	hæl **yūgæd** mæ**kæn** ka**rīb** lil ba**kā'** fih

Phase 3—Finding the trouble

It's up to the mechanic either to find the trouble or to repair it. All you have to do is hand him the book and point to the text in Arabic below.

من فضلك راجع القائمة التالية وأشر الى ما به عيب . واذا أراد الزبون معرفة العيب بالضبط فابحث عن اللفظ المناسب فى القائمة التى تليها (مكسور ، به ماس كهربائى ، الخ . . .)*

فلتر الهواء	air filter
البطارية	battery
البيلا"ت	bearing
علبة السلندرات	block
قفل	bolt
الفرامل	brake
اسطوانة الفرامل [الطمبور]	brake drum
تيل الفرامل [الكوليبه]	brake lining
جهاز هيدروليكية الفرامل	brake hydraulic system

* Please look at the following alphabetical list and point to the defective item. If your customer wants to know exactly what's wrong with it, pick the applicable term from the next list (broken, short-circuited, etc.).

الفرش	brushes
الكابل	cable
عمود الكامة	crankshaft
الكاربراتير	carburettor
قميص السلندر	casing
الهواء	choke
الشاسيه	chassis
الدبرياج	clutch
اسطوانة الدبرياج	clutch plate
البوبينة	coil
الكوندنسر	condenser
عمود اتصال البستم	connecting (piston) rod
التوصيلة	connection
الكونتاكت	contact
جهاز التبريد	cooling system
البيلاّت	crankshaft
الكورونة والترس	crown wheel and pinion
السلندر	cylinder
وجه السلندرات	cylinder head
جوان السلندرات	cylinder head gasket
الغشاء	diaphragm
الدفرنسيال	differential
الدستربيوتر	distributor
أسلاك الدستربيوتر	distributor leads
الدينامو	dynamo (generator)
كهرباء السيارة	electrical system
الموتور	engine
سير المروحة	fan belt
الفلتر	filter
العوامة	float
عجلة القيادة [الدركسيون]	flywheel
عداد/طلمبة/خرطوم/خزان البنزين	fuel gauge/pump/feed/tank
العداد	gauge

gear box	علبة التروس
ignition coil	الاشعال
joint (packing)	جوان
leads	الأسلاك
main bearing	العمود الرئيسى
manifold	ماسورة العادم [الشكمان]
mixture	الخليط [الكاربراتير]
mountings	قواعد الموتور
oil cooler/filter/pump	تبريد/فلتر/طلمبة الزيت
piston	البستم
points	أماكن الاتصال
pump	الطلمبة
radiator	الرادياتير
relay	الرباط
rings	السجمان – حول البستم
rotor arm	شاكوش الدستربيوتر
shaft	عمود
shock-absorber	الأمرتسير
shoes	ماسك الفرامل
silencer (muffler)	ماسورة العادم
sparking plugs	البوجيهات
spring	السوستة [الرفّاص]
starter armature	بوبينة المارش
starter motor	المارش
steering	عجلة القيادة
steering box	علبة عجلة القيادة
suspension	السوست [الرفّاصات]
tappet	القلاّب
teeth	الأسنان
thermostat	الترموستات
timing	توقيت الكهرباء
tracking	زوايا العجل
transmission	عمود الكردان

جوان الكردان	universal joint
البلف [السوباب]	valve
طلمبة الماء	water pump
العجل [الدواليب]	wheels
الأسلاك	wiring

بالقـائمة التـالية بها كلمـات تدل على العيب الموجود فى السيـارة أو ما يلزم عملـه . *

ضبط	to adjust
ضبط الاتزان	to balance
تفريغ	to bleed
مفرقع	blown
مكسور	broken
محترق	burnt
تغيير	to change
شحن	to charge
تنظيف	to clean
به صدأ – متآكل	corroded
مشقوق	cracked
عطلان	defective
وسخ	dirty
غير واصل	disconnected
جـاف	dry
خرط الصبابات	to grind in
عـالى	high
مزنوق	jammed
يخر	leaking
مفكوك	loose
فـك	to loosen
منخفض	low
يقطّع [الموتور]	misfiring

* The following list contains words about what's wrong or what may need to be done with the car.

لا يشحن	not charging
يسخن بشدة	overheating
متآكل	pitted
لعب	play
سريع	quick
تغيير التيلة	to reline
استبدال – تغيير	to replace
الخليط غنى فى الكابراتير	rich
به ماس كهربائى	short-circuited
غير مشدود	slack
ينزلق [يزحط]	slipping
فك الموتور	to strip down
احكام الربط	to tighten
ضعيف	weak
متآكل	worn

Phase 4—Getting it repaired

Have you found the trouble?	هل وجدت العيب ؟	hæl wæ**gædt** æl ēb
Is that serious?	هل هو أمر خطير ؟	hæl **howæ amron** khatīr
Can you repair it?	هل يمكنك اصلاحها ؟	hæl yom**ki**næk islā**ḥ**æhǣ
Can you do it now?	هل يمكنك اصلاحها الآن ؟	hæl yom**ki**næk islā**ḥ**æhǣ æl ′**ǣn**
What's it going to cost?	كم ستتكلف ؟	kæm sætætæ**kæl**læf

What if he says "no"?

Why can't you do it?	لماذا لا يمكنك اصلاحها ؟	**li**mǣzæ lǣ yom**ki**næk islā**ḥ**æha
Is it essential to have that part?	هل هذه القطعة ضرورية ؟	hæl hǣzihi æl **ki**taa darū**ri**yya

How long is it going to take to get the spare parts?	متى يمكن الحصول على قطع الغيار ؟	mætǣ **yom**kin æl ḥos**ū**l æl**ǣ** kit**aa** æl ġiy**ā**r
Where's the nearest garage that can repair it?	أين أقرب جراج يمكنه اصلاحها ؟	æynæ **a**krab gar**āzh** yom**ki**noho isl**ā**ḥæhæ
Can you fix it so that I can get as far as...?	هل يمكنك اصلاحها حتى أصل الى ...	hæl yom**ki**næk isl**ā**ḥæhæ ḥæt**tǣ** asill il**ǣ**

If you're really stuck, ask:

Can I leave my car here for a day/a few days?	هل أستطيع أن أترك سيارتى هنا لمدة يوم / بضعة أيام ؟	hæl astat**ī** æn **a**trok sayy**a**rati **ho**nǣ li**mod**dæt yōm/**bi**daat æyy**ǣm**

CAR—REPAIRS

Settling the bill

Is everything fixed?	هل تم اصلاح كل شيء ؟	hæl **tæm**mæ isl**aḥ** koll shē'
How much do I owe you?	كم الحساب ؟	kæm æl ḥis**ǣb**
Will you take a traveller's cheque?	هل تقبل الشيكات السياحية ؟	hæl **tak**bæl æl shik**ǣt** æl siy**ǣḥiy**yæ
Thanks very much for your help.	شكراً جزيلا على مساعدتك.	**shok**ran gæz**ī**læn æl**ǣ** mos**ǣ**'æda**ti**kæ
This is for you.	هذا لك .	**hǣ**zæ læk

But you may feel that the workmanship is sloppy or that you're paying for work not done. Get the bill itemized. If necessary, get it translated before you pay.

I'd like to check the bill first. Will you itemize the work done?	أريد مراجعة الحساب . من فضلك اكتب تفصيل الشغل .	or**ī**d morag'it æl ḥis**ǣb**. min **fad**lak **ik**tib taf**sīl** æl shogl

If the garage still won't back down–and you're sure you're right—get the help of a third party.

Some Arabic road signs

No U turn

No left turn

No entry

No right turn

Maximum load 10 tons

Maximum speed 60 kph.

Maximum height 4 m.

Maximum width 2 m.

No stopping

Road closed

Parking

No parking

Hospital

No honking

Animal-drawn vehicles prohibited

Handcarts prohibited

اتجاه اجبارى
One way

محطة بنزين
Petrol

ورشة تصليح
Garage

مركز اسعاف ونجدة
First-aid post

مزلقان مفتوح
vel (railroad) crossing without barrier

أقصى عرض
Maximum width 3 m.

أقصى ارتفاع
Maximum height 4 m.

كوبرى متحرك
Opening or swing bridge

مطب
Dip

طريق غير مستو
Uneven road

طريق متعرّج.
Winding road

منحدر خطر
Steep hill

أمامك علامة قف
Stop at major road ahead

تقاطع الطريق
Side road

Location of level (railroad) crossing without gate or barrier

Doctor

Frankly, how much use is a phrase book going to be to you in the case of serious injury or illness? The only phrase you need in such an emergency is...

Get a doctor—quick!	اطلب دكتور – بسرعة !	otlob **doktōr**—bisoraa

But there are minor aches and pains, ailments and irritations that can upset the best planned trip. Here we can help you—and, perhaps, the doctor.

Many doctors will speak English well; others will know enough for your needs. But suppose there's something the doctor can't explain because of language difficulties? We've thought of that. As you'll see, this section has been arranged to enable you and the doctor to communicate. From page 165 to 171, you'll find your side of the dialogue on the upper half of each page; the doctor's is on the lower half.

The whole section has been divided into three parts: illness, wounds, nervous tension. Page 171 is concerned with prescriptions and fees.

General

Can you get me a doctor?	اطلب لى دكتور من فضلك.	otlob li **doktōr** min **fad**lak
Is there a doctor here?	هل يوجد دكتور هنا ؟	hæl **yūgæd doktōr ho**næ
Where's there a doctor who speaks English?	أين يوجد دكتور يتكلم انجليزى ؟	æynæ **yūgæd doktōr** yætæ**kæl**læm ingilīzi
Where's the surgery (doctor's office)?	أين مكتب الدكتور ؟	æynæ **mæk**tæb æl doktōr
What are the surgery (office) hours?	ما هى مواعد العيادة ؟	mææ **hi**yæ mæwæīd æl 'iyææ**dæ**

Could the doctor come to see me here?	هل يستطيع الدكتور الكشف عليّ هنا ؟	hæl yastatī æl doktōr æl kæshf allayya honā
What time can the doctor come?	متى يستطيع الدكتور الحضور ؟	mætæ yastatī æl doktōr æl ḥodūr

Symptoms

Use this section to tell the doctor what's wrong. Basically, what he'll need to know is:

What? (ache, pain, bruise, etc.)
Where? (arm, stomach, etc.)
How long? (have you had the trouble)

Before you visit the doctor find out the answers to these questions by glancing through the pages that follow.

Parts of the body

ankle	قصبة الرجل	kasabit æl rigl
appendix	المصران الأعور	æl mosrān æl 'aawar
arm	ذراع	zirāa
artery	شريان	shoryææn
back	ظهر	zahr
bladder	مثانة	mæsæænæ
blood	دم	dæmm
bone	عظم	azm
breast	ثدى	sædy
chest	صدر	sadr
collar-bone	الترقوة	æl torkowæ
ear	أذن	'ozon
elbow	كوع	kū'
eye	عين	ēn
finger	أصبع	asbaa

foot	قدم	kadam
gland	غدة	goddæ
hand	يـد	yædd
head	رأس	ra's
heart	قلب	kalb
heel	كعب	kææb
hip	ردف	rædf
intestines	مصارين	masarīn
joint	مفصل	mifsal
kidney	كليـة	kilyæ
knee/knee cap	ركبة / صابونة الركبة	rokbæ/sabūnit æl rokbæ
leg	ساق	sæk
liver	كبـد	kæbid
lung	رئـة	ri'æ
mouth	فم	fæm
muscle	عضل	'adal
neck	رقبة	rakabæ
nerve	عصب	'asab
nervous system	الجهاز العصبى	æl gihǣz æl'asabi
nose	أنف	ænf
rib	ضلع	dil'
shoulder	كتف	kitf
skin	الجلد	æl gild
spine	العمود الفقرى	æl 'æmūd æl fakri
stomach	المعدة	æl mi'idæ
tendon	العرقوب	æl 'orkūb
throat	الزور [الزلاعيم]	æl zōr [æl zælǣ'im]
toe	أصبع القدم	asbaa æl kadam
tongue	لسان	lisǣn
tonsils	اللـوز	æl liwæzz
urine	بول	bōl
vein	عرق	'irk
wrist	معصم	mi'sam

PATIENT

Part 1—Illness

I'm not feeling well.	لا أشعر أنى كويس .	læ ash'or ænni kwæyyis
I've got a pain here.	عندى ألم هنا .	indi 'ælæm honæ
His/Her...hurts.	عنده / عندها ألم فى ال...	indo/indæhæ 'ælæm fil
I've got (a)...	عندى ...	indi
headache/backache	صداع / ألم فى الظهر	sodāa/'ælæm fil dahr
fever/sore throat	حرارة / ألم فى الحلق	ḥarāra/'ælæm fil ḥolok
I'm constipated.	عندى امساك .	indi imsæk
I've been vomiting.	عندى قىء .	indi kē'
I feel...	أشعر ...	ash'or
faint/dizzy	بضعف / بدوخة	bidaaf/bidōkhæ
nauseated/shivery	بصداع / برعشة	bisodāa/biraasha

DOCTOR

الجزء الأول – المرض

ما العلة ؟	What's the trouble?
أين الالم ؟	Where does it hurt?
منذ متى وأنت تشعر بهذا الالم ؟	How long have you had this pain?
منذ متى وأنت تشعر بهذا؟	How long have you been feeling like this?
شمر قميصك من فضلك .	Roll up your sleeve.
اخلع ملابسك (حتى الوسط) .	Please undress (down to the waist).
من فضلك اخلع البنطلون واللباس .	Please remove your trousers and underpants.

PATIENT

I've/He's/She's got (a/an) ...	عندى / عنده / عندها...	indi/indo/indæhæ
abscess	دمل	dimmil
asthma	ربو	rabw
boil	خراج	khorrāg
chill	برد	bærd
cold	زكام	zokæm
constipation	امساك	imsæk
convulsions	تشنجات	tæshænnogæt
cramps	شد عضلى	takallosāt
diarrhoea	اسهال	ishæl
fever	حرارة	harāra
haemorrhoids	بواسير	bæwæsīr
hay fever	زكام ربيعى	zokæm rabīi
hernia	فتق	fætk

DOCTOR

ارقد هنا من فضلك .	Please lie down over here.
افتح فمك .	Open your mouth.
تنفس بعمق .	Breathe deeply.
اسعل من فضلك .	Cough, please.
هل هى أول مرة تشعر بهذا ؟	Is this the first time you've had this?
سأقيس درجة حرارتك .	I'll take your temperature.
سأقيص ضغط دمك .	I'm going to take your blood pressure.
سأعطيك حقنة .	I'll give you an injection.
أريد عينة من البول / البراز .	I want a sample of your urine/ stools.
سأصف لك مضاد حيوى .	I'll prescribe an antibiotic.

PATIENT

indigestion	عصر هضم	'osr hadm
inflammation of...	التهاب في ...	'iltihææb fi
influenza	انفلونزا	'ænfilwænzæ
morning sickness	صداع الصباح	sodāa æl sabāḥ
rheumatism	روماتزم	romætizm
stiff neck	التواء فى العنق	'iltiwææ' fil 'onok
sunburn	حرق من الشمس	ḥark min æl shæms
sunstroke	ضربة شمس	darbit shæms
tonsillitis	التهاب فى الزور [الزلاعيم]	'iltihææb fil zōr
ulcer	قرحة	korḥa
whooping cough	سعال ديكى	soææl dīki
It's nothing serious, I hope?	أرجو أن لا يوجد ما يدعو الى القلق .	'argū 'ællæ yūgæd mææ yæd'ū 'ilæl kalak

---

DOCTOR

لا يوجد ما يدعو الى القلق.	It's nothing to worry about.
عندك ...	You've got (a/an)...
حساسية/ التهاب فى الزور [الزلاعيم]	allergy/angina
التهاب فى الزائدة الدودية/ التهاب فى القصبة الهوائية	appendicitis/bronchitis
التهاب فى المثانة / دسنتريا	cystitis/dysentery
تسمم / الصفراء	food poisoning/jaundice
لمباجو / التهاب رئوى	lumbago/pneumonia
التهاب فى ...	an inflammation of...
يجب أن تذهب الى طبيب متخصص .	I want you to see a specialist.
يجب أن تذهب الى المستشفى لاجراء كشف عام .	I want you to go to the hospital for a general check-up.

PATIENT

I'm a diabetic.	عندى مرض السكر .	indi marad æl sokkar
I've a cardiac condition.	أنا مريض بالقلب .	ænǣ marid bil kalb
I had a heart attack in...	أصابتنى ذبحة صدرية فى ...	asābætni zæbḥæ sadriyya fi
I'm allergic to...	عندى حساسية ضد ...	indi ḥæsǣsiyyæ didd
I'd like you to prescribe some medicine for me.	اكتب لى دواء من فضلك.	oktob li dæwǣ' min fadlak
This is my usual medicine.	هذا هو دوائى المعتاد .	hǣzæ howe dæwǣ'i ælmo'tǣd
I need this medicine.	أنا محتاج لهذا الدواء .	ænǣ moḥtǣg li hǣzæ æl dæwǣ
I'm expecting a baby.	أنا حامل .	ænǣ ḥǣmil
Can I travel?	هل يمكنني السفر ؟	hæl yomkinoni æl safar

DOCTOR

ما كمية الانسولين التى تاخذها ؟	What dose of insulin are you taking?
بحقنة أم بالفم ؟	Injection or oral?
ما العلاج الذى تتبعه ؟	What treatment have you been having?
ما الدواء التى تاخذه ؟	What medicine have you been taking?
عندك ذبحة صدرية (خفيفة) .	You've had a (slight) heart attack.
لا نستعمل ... هذا مشابه له جداً .	We don't use... This is very similar.
متى تتوقعين الولادة ؟	When's the baby due?
يجب ألا تسافرى حتى...	You can't travel until...

PATIENT

Part 2—Wounds

Could you have a look at this...?	من فضلك اكشف على هذا / هذه ...	min **fad**lak **ik**shif **æ**læ **hæ**zæ/**hæ**zihi
boil	الخراج	æl khor**rāg**
bruise	الكدمة	æl **kæd**mæ
burn	الحرق	æl **ḥark**
cut	القطع	æl **kat'**
graze	خدش	æl **khædsh**
insect bite	قرصة حشرة	**'ar**sit **ḥa**shara
rash	الطفح	æl **tafḥ**
swelling	الورم	æl **wa**ram
wound	الجرح	æl **gærḥ**
I can't move my...	لا أستطيع أن أحرك ...	**læ** as**ta**tī æn o**ḥær**rik...
It hurts.	انه يؤلمنى .	**in**næho **yo'**limoni

DOCTOR

الجزء الثانى – الجروح

انه (ليس) متلوثا .	It's (not) infected.
عندك انزلاق غضروفى .	You've got a slipped disc.
يجب أن تعمل أشعة .	I want you to have an X-ray.
انه ...	It's...
مكسور / ملتوى	broken/sprained
متحرك من مكانه / متمزق	dislocated/torn
سأصف لك مطهر .	I'll give you an antiseptic.
ليس ما يدعو الى القلق .	It's not serious.
أريد أن تاتى لاراك بعد ... يوم .	I want you to come and see me in... days' time.

DOCTOR

PATIENT

Part 3—Nervous tension

I'm in a nervous state.	أنا في حالة عصبية .	ænǣ fi ḥǣlæ asabiyya
I'm feeling depressed.	أشعر باكتئاب .	ash'or bi'ikti'ǣb
I want some sleeping pills.	أريد حبوباً منومة .	orīd ḥobūbæn monæwwimæ
I can't eat.	لا أستطيع أن آكل .	lǣ astatī æn ǣkol
I can't sleep.	لا أستطيع أن أنام .	lǣ astatī æn ænǣm
I'm having night-mares.	عندي كوابيس .	indi kæwǣbīs
Can you prescribe a...?	من فضلك اكتب لي...	min fadlak iktiblī
sedative/tranquillizer	مسكن / مهدىء	mosækkin/mohæddi'
anti-depressant	مضاد للاكتئاب	modād lil'ikti'ǣb

DOCTOR

الجزء الثالث – التوتر العصبي

عندك اجهاد عصبي .	You're suffering from nervous tension.
انت محتاج الى راحة .	You need a rest.
ما الاقراص التي تتناولها ؟	What pills have you been taking?
كم قرص في اليوم ؟	How many a day?
منذ متى وأنت تشعر بهذا ؟	How long have you been feeling like this?
سأصف لك بعض الاقراص	I'll prescribe some pills.
سأصف لك مسكنا .	I'll give you a sedative.

PATIENT

Prescriptions and dosage

What kind of medicine is this?	ما نوع هذا الدواء ؟	mǣ nōo **hǣ**zæ ældæ**wǣ'**
How many times a day should I take it?	كم مرة فى اليوم يجب أن أتناوله ؟	kæm **mar**ra fil yōm **yæ**gib æn ætæn**ǣwæ**lho
Must I swallow them whole?	هل أبتلعها كاملة ؟	hæl æbtæ**li'**hǣ **kǣ**milæ

Fee

How much do I owe you?	كم يجب أن أدفع لك ؟	kæm **yæ**gib æn **æd**fææ læk
Do I pay you now or will you send me your bill?	هل أدفع لك الآن أم سترسل لى الحساب ؟	hæl **æd**fææ læk æl'**ǣn** æm sæ**tor**sil lī ælḥi**sǣb**
Thanks for your help, doctor.	شكراً على مساعدتك يادكتور .	**shok**ran æ**lǣ** mosǣ'ædætikæ yǣ dok**tōr**

DOCTOR

الجزء الرابع – العلاج والجرعة

خذ ... ملعقة شاى من هذا الدواء كل ... ساعة .	Take...teaspoon(s) of this medicine every ... hours.
خذ ... قرص مع كوب ماء ...	Take...tablets with a glass of water...
... مرة فى اليوم	...times a day
قبل الطعام / بعد الطعام	before each meal/after each meal
فى الصباح / فى المساء	in the mornings/at night

الحساب

الحساب ... من فضلك .	That's...please.
من فضلك ادفع الآن .	Please pay me now.
سأرسل لك الحساب .	I'll send you a bill.

Dentist

Can you recommend a good dentist?	من فضلك انصحنى بطبيب أسنان جيد .	min **fad**lak insaḥnī bitabīb æsnǣn gæyyid
Can I make an (urgent) appointment to see Dr....?	أريد موعداً (عاجلا) مع الدكتور ...	orīd maw'idæn ('ǣgilæn) maal doktōr
Can't you possibly make it earlier than that?	ألا يمكن أن يكون الموعد قبل ذلك ؟	'ælǣ **yom**kin æn yækūn æl **maw**'id kabl zǣlik
I've a toothache.	عندى ألم فى أسنانى .	indī 'ælæm fī æsnǣni
I've an abscess.	عندى خراج .	indī khorrāg
This tooth hurts.	هذه السنة تؤلمنى .	hǣzihi æl **sin**næ to'limoni
at the top	الى أعلى [فوق]	ilǣ 'ææḷǣ [fōk]
at the bottom	الى أسفل [تحت]	ilǣ æsfæl [tæḥt]
in the front	الى الامام	ilǣ æl 'æmǣm
at the back	الى الخلف	ilǣ æl khælf
Can you fix it temporarily?	هل يمكنك علاجها مؤقتاً ؟	hæl yomkinæk ilǣgæhǣ mo'akkatæn
I don't want it extracted.	لا أريد خلعها .	lǣ orīd khæl'ihǣ
I've lost a filling.	سقط حشو السنة .	sakata ḥæshw æl **sin**næ
The gum is...	اللثة ...	æl læsæ
very sore	تؤلمنى بشدة	to' limonī bishiddæ
bleeding	تنزف	tænzif

Dentures

I've broken this denture.	كسرت هذا الطقم .	kasart hǣzæ æl takm
Can you repair this denture?	هل يمكنك اصلاح هذا الطقم ؟	hæl yomkinæk islāḥ hǣzæ æl takm
When will it be ready?	متى يكون جاهزاً ؟	mætǣ yækūn gǣhizæn

Optician

I've broken my glasses.	كسرت نظارتى [عويناتى] .	kasart nazzārati ['owæynæti]
Can you repair them for me?	هل يمكنك اصلاحها ؟	hæl yomkinæk islāḥæhæ
When will they be ready?	متى تكون جاهزة ؟	mætæ tækūn gæhizæ
Can you change the lenses?	هل يمكنك تغيير العدسة؟	hæl yomkinæk tægyīr æl 'ædæsæ
I want tinted lenses.	أريد عدسة غامقة .	orīd 'ædæsæ gæmika
I want contact lenses.	أريد عدسات لاصقة .	orīd ædæsæt lāsika
I'd like to buy a pair of sunglasses.	أريد شراء نظارة شمس.	orīd shirā' nazzārit shæms
I'd like to buy a pair of binoculars.	أريد شراء نظارة معظمة.	orīd shirā' nazzara mo'azzima
How much do I owe you?	كم الحساب ؟	kæm æl ḥisæb
Do I pay you now or will you send me your bill?	هل أدفع لك الآن . أم سترسل لى الفاتورة ؟	hæl ædfæ læk æl'æn æm sætorsil li æl fatūra

FOR NUMBERS, see page 175

Reference section

Where do you come from?

Africa	افريقيا	æfrīka
Algeria	الجزائر	æl gæzǣ'ir
Asia	آسيا	'ǣsyæ
Australia	استراليا	ostralyā
Canada	كندا	kænædæ
Egypt	مصر	misr
Europe	أوروبا	orobba
France	فرنسا	faransa
Great Britain	انجلترا	ingiltirā
Greece	اليونان	æl yonǣn
Ireland	ايرلندا	irlanda
Italy	ايطاليا	italyā
India	الهند	æl hind
Iraq	العراق	æl 'irāk
Jordan	الاردن	æl 'ordon
Lebanon	لبنان	libnǣn
Libya	ليبيا	libyæ
Middle East	الشرق الاوسط	æl shark æl 'awsat
Morocco	المغرب [مراكش]	æl mægrib [marākish]
New Zealand	نيوزيلندا	nyū zilændæ
North America	أمريكا الشمالية	æmrīkæ æl shæmǣliyyæ
Saudi Arabia	السعودية	æl so'ūdiyyæ
South Africa	جنوب افريقيا	gænūb afrikyā
South America	أمريكا الجنوبية	æmrīkæ æl gænūbiyyæ
Sudan	السودان	æl sūdǣn
Syria	سوريا	sūriyyæ
Tunisia	تونس	tūnis
Turkey	تركيا	torkiyæ
USA	الولايات المتحدة	æl wilæyǣt æl mottæḥidæ
USSR	روسيا	rosyǣ

Numbers

٠	0	صفر	sifr
١	1	واحد	wǣḥid
٢	2	اثنين	'itnēn
٣	3	ثلاثة	tælǣtæ
٤	4	أربعة	arbaa
٥	5	خمسة	khæmsæ
٦	6	ستة	sittæ
٧	7	سبعة	sæb'æ
٨	8	ثمانية	tæmǣnyæ
٩	9	تسعة	tisaa
١٠	10	عشرة	ashara
١١	11	أحد عشرة	ḥidāshar
١٢	12	اثنى عشر	itnāshar
١٣	13	ثلاثة عشر	talattāshar
١٤	14	أربعة عشر	arbaatāshar
١٥	15	خمسة عشر	khamastāshar
١٦	16	ستة عشر	sittāshar
١٧	17	سبعة عشر	sabaatāshar
١٨	18	ثمانية عشر	tamantāshar
١٩	19	تسعة عشر	tisaatāshar
٢٠	20	عشرين	'ishrīn
٢١	21	واحد وعشرين	wǣḥid wæ 'ishrīn
٢٢	22	اثنين وعشرين	'itnēn wæ 'ishrīn
٢٣	23	ثلاثة وعشرين	tælǣtæ wæ 'ishrīn
٢٤	24	أربعة وعشرين	arbaa wa 'ishrīn
٢٥	25	خمسة وعشرين	khæmsæ wæ 'ishrīn
٢٦	26	ستة وعشرين	sittæ wæ 'ishrīn
٢٧	27	سبعة وعشرين	sæb'a wæ 'ishrīn
٢٨	28	ثمانية وعشرين	tæmænyæ wæ 'ishrīn
٢٩	29	تسعة وعشرين	tisaa wæ 'ishrīn
٣٠	30	ثلاثين	tælætīn
٣١	31	واحد وثلاثين	wǣḥid wæ tælætīn

٣٢	32	اثنين وثلاثين	'itnēn wæ tælætīn
٤٠	40	أربعين	ærbi'īn
٥٠	50	خمسين	khæmsīn
٦٠	60	ستين	sittīn
٧٠	70	سبعين	sæb'īn
٨٠	80	ثمانين	tæmænīn
٩٠	90	تسعين	tis'īn
١٠٠	100	مائة	miyyæ
١٠١	101	مائة وواحد	miyyæ wæ wǣhid
١١٠	110	مائة وعشرة	miyyæ wæ ashara
١٢٠	120	مائة وعشرين	miyyæ wæ ishrīn
١٥٠	150	مائة وخمسين	miyyæ wæ khæmsīn
١٦٠	160	مائة وستين	miyyæ wæ sittīn
١٧٠	170	مائة وسبعين	miyyæ wæ sæb'īn
١٨٠	180	مائة وثمانين	miyyæ wæ tæmænīn
١٩٠	190	مائة وتسعين	miyyæ wæ tis'īn
٢٠٠	200	مائتين	mitēn
٣٠٠	300	ثلاثمائة	toltomiyyæ
٤٠٠	400	أربعمائة	rob'omiyyæ
٥٠٠	500	خمسمائة	khomsomiyyæ
٦٠٠	600	ستمائة	sittomiyyæ
٧٠٠	700	سبعمائة	sob'omiyyæ
٨٠٠	800	ثمانمائة	tomnomiyyæ
٩٠٠	900	تسعمائة	tos'omiyyæ
١٠٠٠	1,000	ألف	'ælf
١١٠٠	1,100	ألف ومائة	'ælf wæ miyyæ
٥,٠٠٠	5,000	خمسة آلاف	khæmsæt 'ælǣf
١٠,٠٠٠	10,000	عشرة آلاف	asharat 'ælǣf
١٠٠,٠٠٠	100,000	مائة ألف	mit 'ælf
١,٠٠٠,٠٠٠	1,000,000	مليون	milyōn

first	أول	'æwwæl
second	ثانى	t**ǣ**ni
third	ثالث	t**ǣ**lit
fourth	رابع	**rā**bi'
fifth	خامس	**khǣ**mis
sixth	سادس	**sǣ**dis
seventh	سابع	**sǣ**bi'
eighth	ثامن	t**ǣ**min
ninth	تاسع	t**ǣ**si'
tenth	عاشر	'**ǣ**shir
once	مرة	**mar**ra
twice	مرتين	marri**tēn**
three times	ثلاث مرات	tælæt mar**rāt**
a half	نصف	noss
a quarter	ربع	rob'
one third	ثلث	tilt
a pair of	زوج من ...	zōg min
a dozen	دستة [دوزينة]	dæstæ [dozzīnæ]
1980 (year)	١٩٨٠	'ælf wæ tos'**omiy**yæ wæ tæmæ**nīn**
1981	١٩٨١	'ælf wæ tos'**omiy**yæ **wǣ**-hid wæ tæmæ**nīn**
1982	١٩٨٢	'ælf wæ tos'**omiy**yæ 'itnēn wæ tæmæ**nīn**

Time

الثانية عشرة والربع
(it**nā**shar wæ rob′)

الواحدة و ثلث
(**wæḥ**dæ wæ tilt)

الثانية ونصف الا خمسة
(it**nēn** wæ noss **illæ khæmsa**

الثالثة والنصف
(tæ**lǣ**tæ wæ noss)

الرابعة ونصف وخمسة
(arbaa wæ noss wæ **khæmsæ**)

السادسة الا ثلث
(**sit**tæ **il**læ tilt)

السابعة الا الربع
(**sæb**′æ **il**læ rob′)

الثامنة الا عشرة
(**tæ**mæniæ **il**læ ashara)

التاسعة الا خمسة
(**ti**saa **il**læ **khæm**sæ)

العاشرة
(ashara)

الحادية عشرة وخمسة
(ḥi**dā**shar wæ **khæm**sæ)

لثانية عشرة وعشر دقائق
(it**nā**shar wæ ashara)

Have you got the time?

What time is it?	الساعة كم ؟	ælsǣæ kǣm
It's...	الساعة ...	ælsǣæ
Excuse me. Can you tell me the time?	الساعة كم من فضلك ؟	ælsǣæ kǣm min **fad**lak
I'll meet you tomorrow...	سأقابلك غداً ...	sæ'okā**bi**lokæ **gæ**dæn
at 8 o'clock	الساعة الثامنة	ælsǣæ tæ**mæ**nyæ
at 2.30	الساعة الثانية والنصف	ælsǣæ 'it**nēn** wæ nisf
Can I come...?	هل يمكنني الحضور ... ؟	hæl yom**ki**noni ælḥo**dūr**
I'm sorry I'm late.	آسف على التأخير .	'**ǣ**sif 'ælæl tæ'**khir**
At what time does... open/close?	متى يفتح / يقفل ... ؟	**mæ**tā **yæf**tæḥ/**yak**fil
What time will it begin/end?	متى يبدأ / ينتهى ؟	**mæ**tǣ **yæb**dæ'/yæn**tæ**hi
At what time should I be there?	متى يجب أن أصل ؟	**mæ**tǣ **yæ**gib æn '**a**sil
At what time will you be there?	متى ستصل ؟	**mæ**tǣ sæ**ta**sil
after/afterwards	بعد / فيما بعد	**bæ**æd/**fī**mǣ **bæ**æd
before/beforehand	قبل / فيما قبل	kabl/**fī**mǣ kabl
early	مبكراً	mobæk**ki**ran
in time	فى الموعد	fil **mæ**w'id
late	متأخراً	motæ'ækh**khi**ran
midnight	منتصف الليل	mon**ta**saf æl**lēl**
noon	الساعة الثانية عشر ظهراً	æl **sǣ**æ 'it**nā**shar **zoh**ran
hour	ساعة	**sǣ**æ
minute	دقيقة	da**kī**ka
second	ثانية [تكة]	**sǣ**nyæ [**tæk**kæ]
quarter of an hour	ربع ساعة	rob' **sǣ**æ
half an hour	نصف ساعة	nisf **sǣ**æ

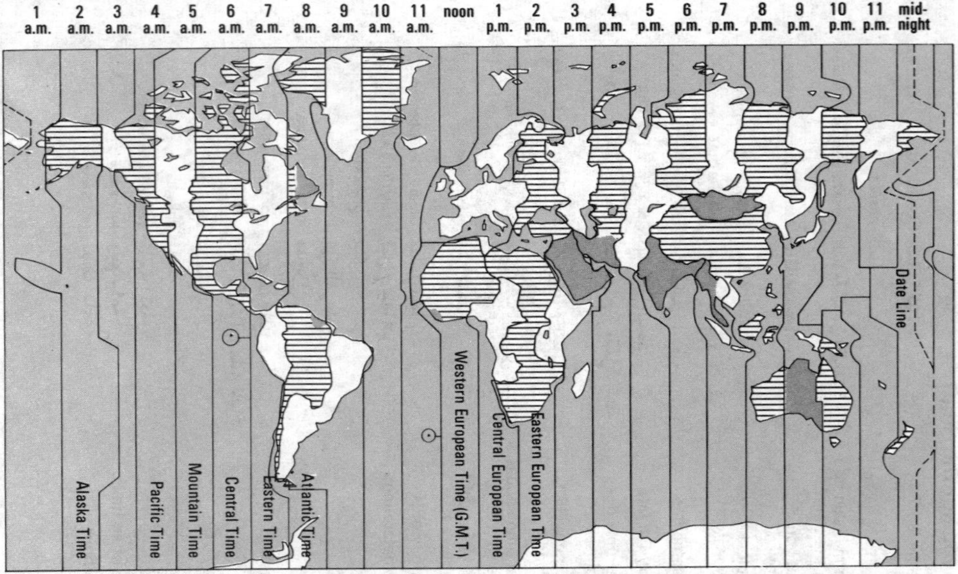

Countries which have adopted a time differing from that in the corresponding time zone. Note also that in the USSR, official time is one hour ahead of the time in each corresponding time zone. In summer, numerous countries advance time one hour ahead of standard time.

Days

What day is it today?	أى الايام اليوم ؟	'æyyil 'ayyǣm æl yōm
Monday	الاثنين	æl 'itnēn
Tuesday	الثلاثاء	æl tælǣt
Wednesday	الاربعاء	æl 'arba'
Thursday	الخميس	æl khæmīs
Friday	الجمعة	æl gom'æ
Saturday	السبت	æl sæbt
Sunday	الاحد	æl 'æḥæd
in the morning	فى الصباح	fil sabāḥ
during the day	خلال اليوم	khilǣl æl yōm
in the afternoon	بعد الظهر	bæædil dohr
in the evening	فى المساء	fil mæsǣ'
at night	فى الليل	fil lēl
yesterday	أمس	'æms
today	اليوم	æl yōm
tomorrow	غداً	gædæn
two days ago	منذ يومين	min yomēn
in three days' time	بعد ثلاثة أيام	bææd tælæt 'æyyǣm
last week	الاسبوع الماضى	æl 'osbū' æl māḍī
next week	الاسبوع القادم	æl 'osbū' æl kādim
birthday	عيد ميلاد	'īd milǣd
day	يوم	yōm
day off	يوم أجازة [فرصة]	yōm 'ægǣzæ [firsa]
holidays	الاجازة [الفرصة]	æl 'ægǣzæ [æl firsa]
month	شهر	shahr
vacation	أجازة [فرصة]	'ægǣzæ [firsa]
week	أسبوع	'osbū'
weekday	يوم فى وسط الاسبوع	yōm fī wistil 'osbū'
weekend	عطلة آخر الاسبوع	'otlit 'ǣkhir æl 'osbū'
working day	يوم عمل	yōm 'æmæl

Months

January	يناير [كانون الثانى]	yænæyir [kænūn æltæni]
February	فبراير [شباط]	fibrāyir [shbāt]
March	مارس [آذار]	mæris [ʼāzār]
April	أبريل [نيسان]	æbrīl [nisæn]
May	مايو [آيار]	mæyo [ʼāyār]
June	يونيو [حزيران]	yonyo [ḥozæyrān]
July	يوليو [تموز]	yolyo [tæmmūz]
August	أغسطس [آب]	ʼagostos [ʼæb]
September	سبتمبر [أيلول]	sibtæmbir [ʼæylūl]
October	اكتوبر [تشرين الاول]	oktōbar [tishrīn æl ʼæwwæl]
November	نوفمبر [تشرين الثانى]	nōvæmbir [tishrīn æl tæni]
December	ديسمبر [كانون الاول]	disæmbir [kænūn æl ʼæwwæl]
since June	منذ شهر يونيو [حزيران]	monzo shahr yonyo [ḥozæyrān]
during the month of August	خلال شهر أغسطس [آب]	khilæl shahr ʼagostos [ʼæb]
last month	الشهر الماضى	æl shahr æl mādī
next month	الشهر القادم	æl shahr æl kādim
July 1	أول يوليو	ʼæwwæl yolyo [tæmmūz]
March 17	السابع عشر من مارس [آذار]	æl sæbii ʼashar min mæris [ʼāzār]

Seasons

spring	الربيع	æl rabīi
summer	الصيف	æl sēf
autumn	الخريف	æl khærīf
winter	الشتاء	æl shitæʼ
in spring	فى الربيع	fil rabīi
during the summer	خلال الصيف	khilæl æl sēf
in autumn	فى الخريف	fil kærīf
during the winter	خلال الشتاء	khilæl æl shitæʼ

Public holidays

Two kinds of calendars are in use in Arab countries. The Gregorian calendar—which is the one we use—is current in normal daily activities. However, newspapers, official documents and certain public holidays follow the Islamic lunar calendar which begins with the Hegira, or emigration of the Prophet Mohammed from Mecca to Medina. 1980 A.D. is the year 1400 of this calendar. The lunar year has twelve months of 29 or 30 days, and thus is approximately 10 days shorter than the Gregorian or solar year.

The names of the Hegira months are:

محرم	mo**ḥar**ram
صفر	**sa**far
ربيع الاول	ra**bī**i æl **'æw**wæl
ربيع الثانى	ra**bī**i æl **tǣ**ni
جمادى الاولى	gæ**mǣ**dæ æl **'ū**lǣ
جمادى الثانية	gæ**mǣ**dæ æl **tæn**yæ
رجب	**ræ**gæb
شعبان	shææ**bǣn**
رمضان	rama**dān**
شوال	shæw**wǣl**
ذو القعدة	zul **ki**ida
ذو الحجة	zul **ḥig**gæ

Given below are the most important Moslem holidays.

1st mo**ḥar**ram	Hegira or Muslim New Year's Day
12th ra**bī**i æl **'æw**wæl	Birth of the Prophet Mohammed
1st to 3th shæw**wæl**	Ramadan Baïram ('id æl fitr) celebrating the end of the holy month of Ramadan which is marked by month-long fasting from sunrise to sunset.
9th to 13th zul **ḥig**gæ	Kurban Baïram ('id æl '**a**dha) celebrating God's mercy toward Abraham in sparing his son; this is the period during which Muslims make a pilgrimage to Mecca.

While there may be additional regional holidays, only national holidays in Egypt (E), Jordan (J) or Lebanon (L) are cited below:

January 1	New Year's Day (Gregorian)		J	L
January 15	Arbor Day		J	
March 8	Syrian Revolution Day	E		
March 22	Founding of the Arab League		J	L
May 1	Labour Day	E	J	L
May 6	Martyr's Day			L
May 25	Independence Day		J	
June 18	Evacuation Day	E		
July 23	Revolution Anniversary	E		
August 11	Accession Day (King Hussein)		J	
August 15	Assumption Day			L
September 1	Libyan Revolution Day	E		
October 6	October War Day	E		
November 1	All Saints' Day			L
November 14	King Hussein's Birthday		J	
November 22	Independence Day			L
December 23	Victory Day	E		
December 25	Christmas Day		J	L
December 31	Foreign Troops Evacuation Day			L
Movable dates:	Good Friday (Catholic or Orthodox)		J	L
	Easter Monday (Catholic or Orthodox)		J	L
	Spring Day, first Monday after Easter	E		

The year-round temperatures

	Amman	Cairo	Beirut
January	39–54 °F	47–65 °F	51–62 °F
February	40–56	48–69	51–63
March	43–60	52–75	54–66
April	49–73	51–83	58–72
May	57–83	63–91	64–78
June	61–87	68–95	69–83
July	65–89	70–96	73–87
August	65–90	71–95	74–89
September	62–88	68–90	73–86
October	57–81	65–86	69–81
November	50–70	58–78	61–73
December	42–59	50–68	55–65

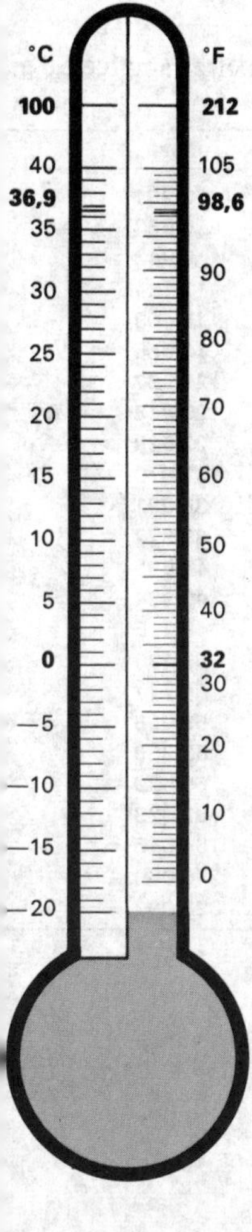

Conversion tables

To change centimetres into inches, multiply by .39.

To change inches into centimetres, multiply by 2.54.

Centimetres and inches

	in.	feet	yards
1 mm	0.039	0.003	0.001
1 cm	0.39	0.03	0.01
1 dm	3.94	0.32	0.10
1 m	39.40	3.28	1.09

	mm	cm	m
1 in.	25.4	2.54	0.025
1 ft.	304.8	30.48	0.305
1 yd.	914.4	91.44	0.914

(32 metres = 35 yards)

Temperature

To convert Centigrade into degrees Fahrenheit, multiply Centigrade by 1.8 and add 32.

To convert degrees Fahrenheit into Centigrade, subtract 32 from Fahrenheit and divide by 1.8.

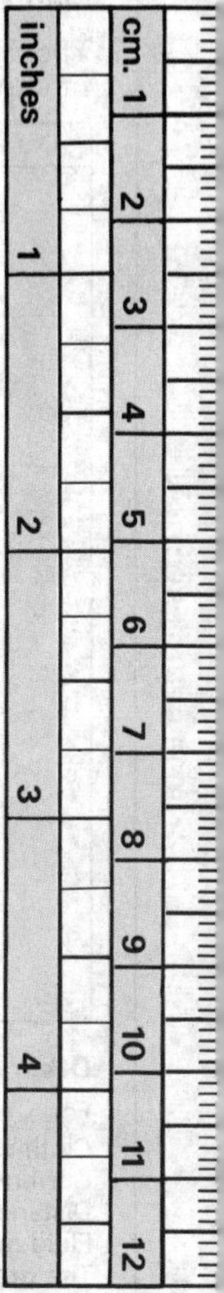

Metres and feet

The figure in the middle stands for both metres and feet, e.g., 1 metre = 3.281 ft. and 1 foot = 0.30 m.

Metres		Feet
0.30	1	3.281
0.61	2	6.563
0.91	3	9.843
1.22	4	13.124
1.52	5	16.403
1.83	6	19.686
2.13	7	22.967
2.44	8	26.248
2.74	9	29.529
3.05	10	32.810
3.35	11	36.091
3.66	12	39.372
3.96	13	42.635
4.27	14	45.934
4.57	15	49.215
4.88	16	52.496
5.18	17	55.777
5.49	18	59.058
5.79	19	62.339
6.10	20	65.620
7.62	25	82.023
15.24	50	164.046
22.86	75	246.069
30.48	100	328.092

Other conversion charts

For	see page
Clothing sizes	115
Currency converter	136
Distance (miles-kilometres)	144
Fluid measures	142
Tire pressure	143

Weight conversion

The figure in the middle stands for both kilograms and pounds, e.g., 1 kilogram = 2.205 1b. and 1 pound = 0.45 kilograms.

Kilograms (kg.)		Avoirdupois pounds
0.45	1	2.205
0.91	2	4.409
1.36	3	6.614
1.81	4	8.818
2.27	5	11.023
2.72	6	13.227
3.17	7	15.432
3.62	8	17.636
4.08	9	19.841
4.53	10	22.045
6.80	15	33.068
9.06	20	44.089
11.33	25	55.113
22.65	50	110.225
34.02	75	165.338
45.30	100	220.450

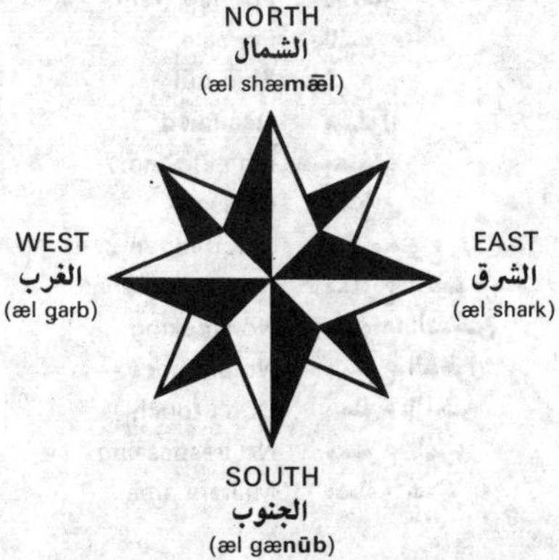

What does that sign mean?

احترس	Caution
احترس من الكلب	Beware of the dog
ادفع	Push
استعلامات	Information
اسحب	Pull
خاص	Private
خالى [فاضى]	Vacant
خروج	Exit
الغزينة	Cashier
خطر	Danger
خطر الموت	Mortal danger
دخول	Entrance
الدخول مجانا	Free entrance
دق الجرس من فضلك	Please ring
رجال	Gentlemen
سيدات	Ladies
طريق خاص	Private road
للايجار	For hire (rent)
للبيع	For sale
مباع	Sold out
مشغول	Occupied
مصعد	Lift (Elevator)
مغلق	Closed
... ممنوع	...forbidden
ممنوع التصوير	No photographs
ممنوع التدخين	No smoking
ممنوع الدخول	No entrance
ممنوع اللمس	Don't touch
ممنوع المرور	No trespassing
منطقة عسكرية	Military area

Emergency!

By the time the emergency is upon you, it's too late to turn to this page to find the Arabic for "I'll scream if you…". So have a look at this list beforehand—and, if you want to be on the safe side, learn the expressions shown in capitals.

Call the police	اطلب البوليس	**'otlob æl bolīs**
CAREFUL	انتبه	'intæbih
Come here	تعالى هنا	tæǣlæ **honǣ**
Come in	ادخل	**'odkhol**
Danger	خطر	**khatar**
Fire	حريق	**ḥærik**
Gas	غاز	gǣz
Get a doctor	اطلب دكتور	**'otlob doktōr**
Get help quickly	اطلب المساعدة بسرعة	**'otlob** ælmosǣ'ædæ bisoraa
Go away	انصرف	'insarif
HELP	النجدة	ælnægdæ
I'm ill	أنا مريض	ænǣ marīd
I'm lost	أنا تهت	ænǣ toht
Keep your hands to yourself	ابعد يدك	'ibiid yædæk
Leave me alone	اتركنى لحالى	'itrokni liḥǣli
Lie down	ارقد	'orkod
Listen	استمع	istæmii
Look	انظر	onzor
LOOK OUT	احترس	iḥtæris
POLICE	بوليس [شرطة]	bōlīs [shorta]
Quick	بسرعة	bisoraa
STOP	قف	kiff
Stop here	قف هنا	kiff honǣ
Stop that man	امسك هذا الرجل	'æmsik hǣzæ æl ragol
STOP THIEF	امسك حرامى	'æmsik ḥarāmi
Stop or I'll scream	قف والا سأصرخ	kif wæ 'illǣ sæ'asrokh

FOR CAR ACCIDENTS, see page 149

Index

Quick reference page

Please/Excuse me.	من فضلك .	min **fad**lak
Thank you.	شكراً .	**shok**ran
Yes/No.	أيوة / لا .	'æywæ/lǣ
I beg your pardon/I'm sorry.	آسف .	'**ǣ**sif
Waiter, please.	من فضلك .	min **fad**lak
How much is that?	بكم هذا ؟	bi**kæm** **hǣ**zæ
Where are the toilets?	أين التواليت ؟	'æynæl twæ**lit**

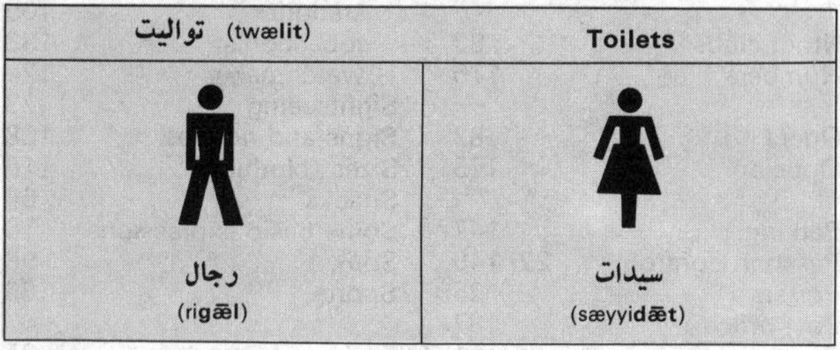
تواليت (twælit)
Toilets
رجال
(rigǣl)
سيدات
(sæyyidǣt)

Help me, please.	ساعدنى من فضلك .	sæ'**id**ni min **fad**lak
What time is it?	الساعة كم ؟	ælsǣæ kǣm
Where's the ... consulate?	اين القنصلية ...	'æynæ sel konsoliyyæ
American	الامريكية	sel'æmrikiyyæ
English	الانجليزية	sel'ingilisiyyæ
What does this mean?	ما معنى هذا ؟	mǣ **mæ**ænǣ **hǣ**zæ
I don't understand.	لا أفهم .	lǣ '**æf**hæm
Just a minute. I'll point out the word.	لحظة . سأشير الى الكلمة .	**laḥ**za. sæ'**oshīr** 'ilæl **kil**mæ
Do you speak English?	هل تتكلم انجليزى ؟	hæl tætæ**kæl**læm ingi**līzi**